dekalog

THE NEW HOME FOR SERIOUS FILM CRITICISM

The *Dekalog* series is a new list of publications dedicated to presenting serious and insightful criticism on a wide range of subjects across the full spectrum of contemporary global cinema.

Each issue is a guest-edited specially themed volume including the writings of a diverse collection of authors, from academic scholars and cultural theorists, film and media critics, and filmmakers and producers, to various personalities involved in all kinds of institutionalised cinephilia such as film festival directors, cinema programmers and film museum curators.

The intention, therefore, is to include the multiple voices of informed and complementary commentators on all things cinematic in dedicated volumes on subjects of real critical interest, especially those not usually served by established periodicals or book-length publications.

ALSO AVAILABLE IN THE *DEKALOG* SERIES:

Dekalog 01: On The Five Obstructions
guest edited by Mette Hjort

Dekalog 02: On Manoel de Oliveira
guest edited by Carolin Overhoff Ferreira

Dekalog 03: On Film Festivals
guest edited by Richard Porton

Dekalog 04: On East Asian Filmmakers
guest edited by Kate Taylor

dekalog⁵
On Dogville

GUEST EDITORS: SARA FORTUNA & LAURA SCURIATTI

WALLFLOWER
LONDON & NEW YORK

A Wallflower Book
Published by
Columbia University Press
Publishers Since 1893
New York • Chichester, West Sussex
cup.columbia.edu

A complete CIP record is available from the Library of Congress

ISBN 978-0-231-16311-8 (pbk. : alk. paper)
ISBN 978-0-231-85019-3 (e-book)

Design by Elsa Mathern

Columbia University Press books are printed on permanent
and durable acid-free paper.
This book is printed on paper with recycled content.
Printed in the United States of America

p 10 9 8 7 6 5 4 3 2 1

Contents

Acknowledgements

We would like to express our gratitude to Signe Iarussi and Katrine Sahl-strøm for their generous help and their constant availability in the long negotiations for organising the interview with Lars von Trier; particularly to Ms Iarussi for her kind hospitality in Zentropa and for providing precious information about *Dogville*. Our most sincere thanks also go to Mr von Trier for accepting to have with us a long, very insightful and friendly conversation, and to Yoram Allon at Wallflower Press for encouraging us to persist in our attempt to talk to Mr von Trier in spite of what looked like almost insurmountable difficulties. We would also like to thank our colleagues and students for sharing the enthusiasm for our project.

We are very grateful to Batholomew Ryan for his comments, his care and patience in revising the manuscript and his readiness to devote himself to this project even during his journey through the Indian subcontinent.

Finally we want to express our gratitude to all of those who in many different ways with their comments, intellectual engagement and curiosity supported our project and contributed to its success.

Notes on Contributors

Brunella Antomarini (PhD in Aesthetics at Gregoriana University in Rome, teaches Aesthetics and Contemporary philosophy at John Cabot University in Rome) is the author of the volumes *Pensare con l'errore* (2008), *L'errore del maestro* (2006), *La percezione della forma in Hans Urs von Balthasar* (2004). A selection of her recent publications includes:'Teatri dell'occhio. L'alternarsi non-lineare delle teorie dei colori', in Licata I. (ed.), *Connessioni inattese. Crossing tra arte e scienza*; 'La natura come caso speciale della tecnica' (2007), in *Il corpo e la tecnica* (ed. with S Tagliagambe); *The Notion of Afterlife in Benjamin's Philosophy of History. Proceedings of the International Conference at John Cabot University on Critical Theory* (2007); 'The Acoustical Pre-history of Poetry' (2004), *New Literary History*.

Sergio Benvenuto (Philosopher and psychoanalyst, Researcher at the National Research Council in Rome, Italy) is president of Institute for Advanced Studies in Psychoanalysis. He is a contributor to cultural journals such as *Telos, Lettre Internationale* (German, French, Spanish and Italian editions), *Texte, RISS, Journal for Lacanian Studies, L'évolution psychiatrique*. He translated Jacques Lacan's *Séminaire XX: Encore* into Italian. His books include *Dicerie e pettegolezzi* (1999); *Un cannibale alla nostra mensa* (2000,'A Cannibal at Our Table. Relativist Arguments in the Era of Globalization'); *Perversioni. Sessualità, etica, psicoanalisi* (2005; 'Perversions. Sexuality, Ethics, Psychoanalysis'); *Accidia. La passione dell'indifferenza* (2008), *On Freud's Tracks* (2008, with A. Molino).

Carmen Dell'Aversano (University of Pisa; European Institute of Sistemic Therapy, Milan; Institute of Constructivist Psychology, Padua). Her main research interests are literary theory and criticism, rhetorics, animal studies, radical constructivism, personal construct psychology, and the epistemology of the human and social sciences. Some of her most recent publications are *La scrittura argomentativa* ('Writing Arguments', with Alessandro Grilli, 2005); 'Beyond Dream and Reality: Surrealism as Reconstruction' (2008) in *Journal of Constructivist Psychology*; *L'analisi posizionale del testo letterario* ('The Positional Analysis of Literary Texts', 2009); 'The Love whose Name Cannot be Spoken: Queering the Human-Animal Bond' (2010). She is currently focusing on the application of methodologies from the social sciences to the interpretation of literary texts and on the ways social and cultural phenomena can be elucidated through concepts drawn from literary theory.

Astrid Deuber-Mankowsky (Media Studies, Gender Studies; Ruhr University, Bochum, Germany) has published numerous studies on gender theory, philosophy, in particular on Walter Benjamin, and media. Amongst her recent publications are: *Lara Croft. Cyber Heroine* (2005); *Der frühe Walter Benjamin und Hermann Cohen. Jüdische Werte. Kritische Philosophie. Vergängliche Erfahrung* (2000; 'The Early Walter Benjamin and Hermann Cohen. Jewish Values, Critical Philosophy, Transient Experience'); *Praktiken der Illusion* (2007).

Sara Fortuna (Philosophy of Language at the Università Guglielmo Marconi; associate member at the Berlin Institute for Cultural Inquiry) has worked on theories of physiognomics, perception and origin of language as well as on aesthetics, feminist theories, films. Her publications include *A un secondo sguardo* (2002); *Il laboratorio del simbolico: Fisiognomica, percezione, linguaggio da Kant a Steinthal* (2005); *The Power of Disturbance: Elsa Morante's 'Aracoeli'* (2009; ed. with M. Gragnolati); *Dante's Plurilingualism* (2010; ed. with M. Gragnolati and J. Trabant); *Il giallo di Wittgenstein* (2010).

Maximilian de Gaynesford (Professor of Philosophy at the University of Reading) is the author of *I: The Meaning of the First Person Term* (2006);

Hilary Putnam (2006); *John McDowell* (2004) and of papers on Metaphysics, the Philosophy of Mind and Language, Poetry and the Philosophy of Film. He is currently working on the concept of integrity in moral philosophy and on the relationship between poetry and philosophy.

Laura Scuriatti (Junior Professor of Literature at ECLABard, a Liberal Arts University in Berlin, Germany) works on Anglo-American and Italian modernism, gender theory and the relationship between literature, art and architecture. She has published articles on H. G. Wells, Ford Madox Ford, Mina Loy and on gender construction and representation in film, contemporary art and advertising. She edited the anthology of contemporary German literature *Berlin Babylon* (2004), she is the co-editor of *The Exhibit in the Text: The Museological Practices of Literature* (2009), and is currently working on a monograph on the poet and artist Mina Loy.

Preface

SARA FORTUNA & LAURA SCURIATTI

From the moment of their release, the films of Lars von Trier have reliably become the stuff of heated debates, not only amongst the cinephiles and the academics, but also for a broad and differentiated public across the world. They have been discussed, loathed and loved on the pages of newspapers, on internet forums, printed and digital magazines and in university classrooms.[1] They invariably disturb, stir controversy and stimulate thought. They generate extreme and contradictory reactions, as if these films, both singularly and as a corpus, were able to always strike a painful but titillating chord – a perplexing and highly disturbing ability, perhaps best summed up by the impatience of a smart colleague of ours, a famous Italian feminist philosopher working in the USA, who, a couple of years ago, exclaimed that Lars von Trier should, for everybody's sake, stop producing masterpieces!

This is, indeed, what prompted us to commit to this project, initially generated by the realisation that *Dogville* had become for many of us the basic text for discussing as teachers, intellectuals and citizens, some of the most interesting and fundamental issues concerning politics, philosophy, aesthetics, ethics and religion. Once we started our research on the subject, we realised that we were not alone in having found in *Dogville* an almost inexhaustible source of ideas and intellectual tools, and that the range of people debating the film did by no means consist of the usual suspects, which, according to many, have become the privileged and restricted public of so-called arthouse cinema.

So what makes this film so interesting and controversial? We will leave the task of addressing the complexity of the film and the multiple layers of meanings and questions it raises to the chapters in this volume; but before leaving the stage to our authors, it might be useful to outline some of the main informative elements of this successful and controversial film. In doing so we also intend to adopt the format of the first *Dekalog* volume on Lars on Trier's and Jørgen Leth's *The Five Obstructions*, 'providing relevant (contextual) information that will further enhance the viewers' experience of the films' (Mette Hjort).

Credits

Dogville, 2003
Director: Lars von Trier
Script: Lars von Trier
Music: Antonio Vivaldi, Tomaso Albinoni, Georg-Friedrich Händel, Giovanni Battista Pergolesi, David Bowie
Director of Photography: Anthony Dod Mantle
Montage: Molly Marlene Stensgård
Production design: Peter Grant
Actors: Nicole Kidman (Grace Margaret Mulligan), Harriet Anderson (Gloria), Lauren Bacall (Ma Ginger), Jean-Marc Barr (the man with a hut), Paul Bettany (Tom Edison), Blair Brown (Mrs. Henson), James Caan (the tall man), Patricia Clarkson (Vera), Jeremy Davies (Bill Henson), Ben Gazzara (Jack McKay), Philip Baker Hall (Tom Edison Sr.), Siobhan Fallon (Martha), Zeljko Ivanek (Ben), Udo Kier (the man with a coat), Cleo King (Olivia), Miles Purinton (Jason), Bill Raymond (Mr. Henson), Chloë Sevigny (Liz Henson), Shauna Shim (June), Stellan Skarsgård (Chuck)
End credit photos by: Jacob Holdt/American Pictures; Pol Foto/ Nixon; Jim Jubbard/American Refugees; Douglas A. Harper/Good Company; Dan Holmberg/Nye Scener Fra Amerika. From the Library

of Congress, Prints & Division, FSA – OWI Collection: photographs by Russel Lee, Dorothea Lange, Jack Collier, A. Siegel, Carl Mydans, J. Vachon, Arthur Rothstein

Awards

Bodil Awards (2004), Best Film, Lars von Trier
Cinema Brazil Grand Prize (2005), Best Foreign Film
Cinema Writers Circle Awards (Spain), CEC Award (2004), Best Foreign Film
Copenhagen International Film Festival, Honorary Award (2003), Lars von Trier
David di Donatello Awards, David (2004), Best European Film, Lars von Trier
European Film Award (2003) Best Cinematographer Anthony Dod Mantle (also for *28 Days Later*)
Guild of German Art House Cinemas (2004) Guild Film Award – Silver, Foreing Film
Robert Festival (2004), Best Costume Design, Manon Rasmussen
Robert Festival (2004), Best Screenplay, Lars von Trier
Russian Guild of Film Critics, Golden Aries (2003), Best Foreign Actress, Nicole Kidman
Russian Guild of Film Critics, Golden Aries (2003), Best Foreign Film
Sofia International Film Festival, Audience Award (2004), Best Film, Lars von Trier

Nominations

Bodil Awards (2004), Best Actress, Nicole Kidman
Bodil Awards (2004), Best Supporting Actor, Stellan Skarsgård
Cannes Film Festival Golden Palm (2003), Lars von Trier
Chlotrudis Awards (2005), Best Cast, Best Screenplay, Lars von Trier
César Awards France, César (2004), Best European Union Film, Lars von Trier
European Film Award (2003), Audience Award, Best Director, Lars von

Trier
European Film Award (2003), Best Director, Lars von Trier
Golden Trailer Awards (2005), Best Independent
Goya Awards (2004), Best European Film
Guldbagge Awards (2004), Best Foreign Film
Italian National Syndicate of Film Journalists (2004), Silver Ribbon, Best Director – Foreign Film
Robert Festival (2004), Best Cinematography, Anthony Dod Mantle
Robert Festival (2004), Best Director, Lars von Trier
Robert Festival (2004), Best Editing, Molly Marlene Stensgård
Robert Festival (2004), Best Film, Vibeke Windelov (producer), Lars von Trier (director)
Robert Festival (2004), Best Pruction Design, Peter Grant
Robert Festival (2004), Best Supporting Actor, Stellan Skarsgård

CD Soundtrack and DVD editions of the film

Soundtrack of Dogville *and* Manderlay
Date of release: 2006
Label: Victor
Contents:
Dogville Overture – A. Vivaldi, *Concert in G major*
Thoughts of Tom – G.-F. Händel, *Concerto Grosso in D major*
Happy at Work – T. Albinoni, *Concert for Oboe in D minor*
Dogville Theme – A. Vivaldi, *Concert in G major*
The Gifts – A. Vivaldi, *Concert for Flute in D minor*
Happy Times in Dogville – T. Albinoni, *Concert for Oboe in D minor*
Fast Motion – A. Vivaldi, *Concert in G Major*
The Fog – A. Vivaldi, *Madrigalesco RV 139*
Grace Gets Angry – A. Vivaldi, *Nisi Dominus RV 608*
Change of Time – G. B. Pergolesi, *Stabat Mater*
Manderlay Theme – A. Vivaldi, *Concert for Basson in A minor*
Mam's Death – A. Vivaldi, *Concert in G minor*
The Child – A. Vivaldi, *Al Santo Sepolcro* and *Quando Corpus Morietur*
The Swallows Arrives – G.-F. Händel, *Aria*

David Bowie, *Young Americans*

Extra materials in different DVD editions
Dogville Confessions. Documentary by Sami Saif who followed Lars von Trier, Nicole Kidman and Stellan Skarsgård around and interviewed them (53 minutes)
- Trier and Kidman (Cannes, 23 minutes)
- The *Dogville* Test. A test of the setting with actors Nikolai Lee Kaas and Sidse Babett Knudsen (6 minutes)
- Audio commentary of the film by Lars von Trier and Anthony Dod Mantle
- Interviews with: Nicole Kidman (6 minutes), Nicole Kidman (4 minutes), Stellan Skarsgård (7 minutes), Anders Refn (6 minutes), Lars von Trier (20/05/03, Cannes, 5 minutes), Lars von Trier (23/05/03, Cannes, 5 minutes)
- Deleted Scenes from *Dogville Confessions* (18 minutes)
- Visual effects (8 minutes, with audio commentary by Peter Hjort)
- *Dogville* visuals (poster, artworks, storyboards)
- Press conference Trollhättan (10 minutes)
- Press conference Cannes (10 minutes)
- Lars von Trier meets the Danish press (3 minutes)
- Interview by Coming Soon TV with Lars von Trier (7 minutes) and a videoconference (37 minutes) realized when the film was released in Italy.
- Video reportage about FilmByen, the Danish town of cinema of which Von Trier's Zentropa is a part (20 minutes)
- Trailers in English and other languages

Adaptations for the theatre

Dogville
Adaptation: Christian Lollike
Premiered in February 2008, Stadttheater Bremerhaven

Stadttheater Fürth, June 2007

Adaptation: Christian Lollike
Director: Jochen Schölch
Scenography: Jochen Schölch, Christl Wein

Premiered on 15 September 2006 Volkstheater Wien
Adaptation: Christian Lollike
Director: Georg Schmiedleitner

World premiere in German language: Autumn 2005, Staatstheater
   Stuttgart
Premiered on 17 December 2004, Athens National Theatre
Director: Volker Lösch
Scenography: Carola Reuther
Director: Antons Kalogridis

Dogville
Adaptation: Karel František Tománek
Translation: Dana Hábová
Director: Miroslav Krobot
National Theatre, Prague, Premiere June 2010
Lars von Trier, *Dogville*, trans. into German by Maja Zade, adapted by
   Christian Lollike, Rowohlt Theaterverlag

Grace was here
Playwright: Christian Lollike in collaboration with Mads Madsen and
   Cecilie Schmidt
Director: Christian Lollike
Scenography: Marco Evaristti
Premiered at Mammutteatret, Copenhagen 2007

NOTES

1   A long list of reviews of the film can be found at: www.imdb.com/title/tt0276919/externalreviews. For other stimulating studies on *Dogville* which have not been quoted in the volume, see: S. Orth, M. Steiger and J. Valentin (eds) (2008) *'Dogville'-Godville. Methodische Zugänge zu einem Film Lars von Triers*. Marburg: Schüren Verlag; M. Rovelli (2009) *'Dogville* di Lars von Trier', in P. Antonello and E. Bujatti (eds) *La violenza allo specchio. Passione e sacrificio nel cinema contemporaneo*. Massa: Transeuropa, 117–20; W. Staat (2007) *'Dogville* Characterized by *The Grapes of Wrath*: European Identity Construction through American Genre Conventions', *The Journal of Cinema and Media*, 48, 1, 79–96.

Dogville and the Problem of Objectification

LAURA SCURIATTI

Die Welt ist arm, der Mensch ist schlecht
Wir wären gut – anstatt so roh
Doch die Verhältnisse, sie sind nicht so
– Bertold Brecht

(The world is poor, and man's a shit
We should aim high instead of low
But our condition's such it can't be so)

In the opening scene of *Dogville*, an omniscient third-person narrator speaking in a suave voice and impeccable British accent (actor John Hurt) introduces Tom's literary and intellectual endeavours to the spectators with a mocking metaphor:

> 'And if a body found it hard to grasp what profession he was busy at he'd merely reply "mining". For although he did not blast his way through rock he blasted through what was even harder … namely the human soul … right into where it glistered!'

The occurrence of this metaphor strikes me not only for being trite and for exposing Tom's ambitions as banal and unrealistic, but most of all because it creates a figurative traffic around the actual mine in Dogville, an abandoned area which is shown at the very beginning of the film, and which serves as a shelter for Grace once Tom has discovered her. In the first few minutes of the film we are presented with a place which becomes metaphor which becomes place in which the metaphor may in turn become materially true. If Grace is a gift to Dogville, the first manifestation of this gift is that she hides in the mine, thus offering the possibility that Tom's work, expressed in terms of 'mining', may come true. The very first scenes of the film are also characterised by this tension between the possibility of literal and metaphorical readings. The brief exchange between Tom and Chuck about Moses, Dogville's dog, are exemplary in this sense:

Chuck: Moses was meant to be hungry! To keep watch.
Tom: Keep watch in Dogville? What's there to steal?

The figurative overload around the figure of the dog with its biblical name and its task of keeping watch over Dogville is immediately tamed by Tom's sceptical questions, which reduces the ambiguity of Chuck's utterance to the sheer fact of Dogville's material poverty. Does Tom's reply mean to warn the spectators to the dangers of (mis)interpretation, of an overly literary mode of reception of the film? Perhaps. But this brief exchange could also be alerting us to the fact that Tom's mode of thinking may be a little too materialistic.

The point I want to make in drawing attention to these two initial moments in the film is that *Dogville* is concerned with the issue of the relationship between abstract concepts and material things, with the multiple and complex mechanisms by which the former ones are figuratively associated to the latter, and the problematic status of things, once they have become the signs and embodiments of concepts and ideas, as well as the main targets of desire. An aspect which is connected to this problem in the film is, in turn, how objects become the paradigm for any relationship between persons. This concern informs the whole film, which has at its very core a most prominent example of these relationships, namely with the character of Grace, whose name denotes an abstract quality, which the film leads us to identify with divine Grace, a gift by God to human beings, as much as Grace is presented as a 'gift to Dogville'. Clearly, the film and its tragic plot presents the reduction of an individual to an abstract quality as a problem, with the complication that Grace's offering herself metaphorically as a 'gift' to the village is taken literally by Dogville's inhabitants, who effectively turn her into an object, or a series of objects, which can be used and exploited by the entire population, leading to the tragic moral downfall of the town and its elimination.

It is therefore on the question of objectification that I would like to focus in my reading of the film, which does not claim to be exhaustive or definitive. Indeed, as the range and efficacy of the following contributions to the film and the relatively large amount of literature devoted to the film suggest, *Dogville* presents itself as an almost inexhaustible text, allowing for a number of convincing and politically as well as philosophically relevant readings which nevertheless do not fully account for its complexity and troubling quality.

1. Objectification and its discontent

For now I will define 'objectification' simply as the way in which a person is treated as a thing. The term, which recurs in Marxist and Feminist writings, is almost exclusively intended to have pejorative connotations, although, as Martha Nussbaum observes in her critical reading of Catharine MacKinnon and Andrea Dworkin's works, this should not be intended as being so by default (Nussbaum 1995). Objectification is often also given as a synonym for 'reification', a term (from the Latin *res*, *rei*: 'thing', 'business', 'affairs' and *facio*: 'make') that translates the German word *Verdinglichung* (*Ding* meaning 'thing'), and is mainly, although not exclusively, associated with Marxist theory and thought. At the beginning of his essay 'Reification and the Consciousness of the Proletariat', Georg Lukács defines reification as ultimately coterminous with the phenomenon of commodity fetishism analysed by Marx in *Das Kapital*, suggesting that the basis for the commodity-structure is 'that a relation between people takes on the character of a thing and thus acquires a "phantom objectivity", an autonomy that seems so strictly rational and all embracing as to conceal every trace of its fundamental nature: the relation between people' (1971: 83).[1] Reification therefore implies a deep misunderstanding, indeed a misapprehension of reality, so that whatever pertains to the sphere of human relations is seen to have a life of its own, independent of the persons involved. In Lukács's account, what is specifically reified is human labour and its products (not restricted to industrial or agricultural production), which are perceived as 'something objective and independent of [the worker], something that controls him by virtue of an autonomy alien to man' (1971: 87). Labour is therefore mistakenly thought of as being embodied by material products which are entirely subject to the forces of the market, and, according to the author, in advanced capitalism this extends to all aspects of human life, which are rationalised and reified, such as, for example, time:

'thus time sheds its qualitative, variable, flowing nature; it freezes into quantifiable "things" (the reified, mechanically objectified performance of the worker, wholly separated from his human personality)' (1971: 90)

So much so that human beings become 'incarnations of time', insofar as 'one man during an hour is worth just as much as another man during an hour' (1971: 89). Once quantity systematically substitutes quality in this way and every aspect of human life is affected by this paradigm, people are robbed of their agency and responsibility, as they are unable to think of any of their activities as connected to them.[2]

I want to suggest that this may be useful in understanding the sequence of events following Grace's arrival in the township of Dogville. From the very beginning of the film, Grace's stay in the village is predicated upon her working for free for the inhabitants in order to get them to appreciate her, so that they would agree to host her and ultimately hide her from her persecutors. Saving Grace's life, and even 'liking her', as Jason, Vera and Chuck's child, cynically stresses, immediately requires a *quid pro quo* – as Tom will put it, later on in the film, when keeping Grace is revealed to be more dangerous, and Grace's output proportionally more expensive – a paradoxical exchange whereby Grace buys through her unpaid work the possibility of: i) giving herself wholly to Tom and the village; ii) giving herself as a present (Tom defining her a 'gift'; she is supposed to offer things that are not necessary, but one would want done anyway – that is, presents); and iii) being hidden and staying alive. Under these circumstances, Dogville's 'problem of acceptance' (affecting Tom as anybody else) seems to involve not only the inability to accept that things may be given to them, or to accept anybody alien to their community, but, more fundamentally, that accepting means precisely giving up the urge to quantify anything offered and to turn it into an object for economic transaction. The narrator doesn't fail to emphasise and expose this paradox at a point when the film seems to paint a picture of harmony, prior to the first major change of attitudes and circumstances that will bring about a worsening of Grace's situation and an increase in the sadism of the inhabitants of the village: 'Grace had bared her throat to the village and they had given her a gift: friendship.'

The description of Grace's integration in the life of the village which follows this statement betrays a rather disconcerting situation: Grace 'could serve as eyes for McKay, a mother for Ben, as friends for Vera and brains for Bill' and eventually 'received wages, not much but enough to save up for the first of the tiny china figurines … in the window of the store. And she dreamed that in time she would be able to acquire them all'. Grace is slowly rationalised and dismembered into a series of functions and tools, as if her work had nothing to do with herself as a person, with her as a whole individual. One is compelled to ask whether in this case friendship, a feeling of love or affection for somebody strictly for their own sake, may really be experienced and given by the inhabitants of Dogville. Grace's response is similarly flawed: her desire to win the friendship (beyond her need of protection) of the Dogvillians takes once again the form of an economic transaction, the 'acquisition' of the little figurines, objects that figuratively stand for the community.

It is precisely the reciprocal, constant and inescapable objectification of the other which introduces the possibility of exploitation on one side, and of the resignation to the lack of responsibility, on the other. If for Grace the Dogvillians are like the figurines – naïve and kitschy little figures which can be bought at the cost of some hard labour and can be made to show their good will and appreciation – this may be seen as part of Grace's arrogance, which leads her to see the Dogvillians as exotic beings ultimately devoid of real agency and knowledge, exempting them from the application of accepted moral standards. On the other hand, the system in which Grace's labour is defined and exchanged eventually and increasingly prevents Dogville's inhabitants to conceive of her as a person, and therefore to treat her as such.

After the Fourth of July celebrations this paradigm becomes even clearer. Grace's status as a fugitive has changed and so is the attitude of Dogville towards her. As Tom put it: 'From a business perspective your presence has become more costly because it has become more dangerous to have you here: there has to be some *quid pro quo.*' This turns out to involve Grace having to visit each household twice, instead of once a day, in half-hour slots, and a lowering of her wages. The church bell will chime every half hour to mark the end and the beginning of a new shift for Grace, who has indeed, as indicated by Lukács's analysis, been reduced to her labour and to abstract quantities of time. Once this paradigm emerges in its bare form, although its increasing strength and pervasiveness is proportionally clad in hypocritical jargon, there is no limit to the forms of exploitation to which Grace is submitted. If Chuck still tried to redefine his rape of Grace in terms of respect and friendship, Ben, the notorious frequenter of prostitutes in the film, is adamant that 'it's not personal, I have to take due payment' because 'if this was a professional job, it would be called a surcharge for dangerous goods'. Ben's refusal to take responsibility for his raping Grace is made possible by the depersonalisation brought about by the economic subtext of objectification.

In her illuminating analysis of the phenomenon of objectification, Martha Nussbaum suggests that in order to be properly understood and assessed, objectification needs to be considered as consisting of seven different aspects, who are not all necessarily logical consequences of one another, and may not occur simultaneously: *instrumentality* ('the objectifier treats the object as a tool for his/her own purposes'), *denial of autonomy* and self-determination, *inertness* (the object is treated as 'lacking in agency'), *fungibility* (the object is seen as being potentially interchangeable with others of the same type), *violability* (the object is treated as 'lacking in boundary integrity'), *ownership, denial of subjectivity* ('the objectifier treats the object as something whose experience and feelings need not be taken into account') (1995: 257).

Nussbaum argues that, amongst the various aspects of objectifications, the one that seems most crucial for understanding the dire effects of objectification is instrumentality. Quite convincingly, she shows that 'there is something especially problematic about' treating somebody '*primarily* or *merely* as instruments', that is,

'something that involves denying what is fundamental to them as human beings, namely, the status of being ends in themselves. From this one denial, other forms of objectification that are not logically entailed in the first seem to follow. [...] The very decision to treat a person as not an end in him- or herself, but as a mere tool, leads rather naturally to a failure of imagination. Once one makes that basic move it is very easy indeed to stop asking the questions morality usually dictates, such as What is this person likely to feel if I do X? What does this person want, and how will my doing X affect her with respect to those wants? And so on' (1995: 265).

For Nussbaum the typical and most extreme manifestation of the treatment of persons as mere tools is slavery – a subject that clearly informs the first two parts of the 'Land of Opportunities' trilogy, *Dogville* and *Manderlay* (2005) in a staggering progression. In the former, Grace is progressively enslaved, as her work, initially paid for, is then blatantly forced upon her; similarly and in parallel, Dogvillians increasingly appropriate her body and turn her into a sexual slave, precisely through what Nussbaum identifies as a 'failure of imagination', which prevents the inhabitants from considering Grace in terms of her feelings, needs and suffering, rather than just as a mere aggregate of instruments. However, the dehumanisation of Grace is also made possible through, and confirmed by, her own acquiescence to abuses: her passivity, her failure to activate even the most primitive mechanisms of self-defence, her readiness to see herself as separated from her own body,[3] may be seen as a renunciation on Grace's own part of the basic aspects of human identity[4] – a renunciation which she shares with the anti-heroines and protagonists of the trilogy. Grace's attempt to understand and undo the established slave community in *Manderlay* suggests, however, that Grace, unlike Dogville's inhabitants, and in spite of the problematic ending of the film where she seems to adopt their pseudomorality, does not suffer from the failure of imagination which led to her own subjection to slavery. She is led, by chance, to do exactly the opposite: to immerse herself in a community where, by definition, everybody's legal status is that of a mere instrument. In this sense, *Manderlay* may be seen as discarding the quietism which affected Grace and ultimately *Dogville* itself until the end.

2. *Dogville* as a critique of the USA?

Grace's acquiescence is interesting in more than one way. It seems to me that her figure embodies a critique of a specific cultural stereotype of femininity (especially common in nineteenth-century culture and in Christian morality), constructed as an (unattainable) aggregate of virtues – purity, renunciation, acquiescence, tolerance, selflessness, innocence – leading to both masochism and arrogance; and in this sense *Dogville* forces us to critically reconsider the 'Golden Heart' trilogy in this light.

Lars von Trier has explicitly declared that the trajectory of Grace's subjection and final act of revenge and liberation was inspired by the song of Pirate Jenny in Bertold Brecht's *Dreigroschenoper* (Threepenny Opera, 1928).[5] In Brecht's play the song is performed by Polly Peachum, the daughter of the boss of the London beggars, at her secret wedding with gangster boss Macheath (Mackie). In the song, Jenny, who washes the dishes and scrubs the floors in a cheap hotel, sings about a pirate ship which will come and free her from her drudgery; nobody in town really knows who she is and therefore they take advantage of her, but once the pirate ship will have appeared on the horizon Jenny's face will light with a mischievous smile. The ship will fire cannon balls against the town, destroying it, all but the crumbling hotel where Jenny works, and once the pirates will have entered town, they will ask Jenny whom to kill, and she will answer: 'all!' Jenny is also the name of a character in the play, a prostitute which was once Macheath's lover, and who betrays him to the police for money, in order to please Mr and Mrs Peachum, who resent him marrying their daughter. Like Pirate Jenny, Polly is associated with the criminals and ultimately depends on them; Polly, however, represents the counterpart of Jenny, as she, like Grace, rebels against her father and ultimately ends up running the gangster band with a fist of iron while Macheath is in jail. Jenny's song, originally performed by Lotte Lenya, has become very successful, also for its supposedly revolutionary subtext.[6] Most readers, however, agree in interpreting the song as a fantasy of liberation, dreamed up by poor Jenny, who clearly will never be freed from her slavery. Jenny's fantasy produces a striking contrast with the solidity and hypocrisy of a social order in which injustice, exploitation, corruption and robbery are integrated and masked by a terminology borrowed from the jargon of economics and business, as Werner Hecht observes: beggars, robbers and prostitutes and their allegiances are defined with terms such as 'companies', 'banks', 'businesses', 'enterprises' and 'marriages' (1995: 210). The ironic relationship between the two realms in the play clearly both unmasks the self-declared respectability of the criminals in the play, but also undermines the ethics and morality of the bourgeois and capitalist social order based on such institutions. As shown above, this is also a subtext in *Dogville*, where the injustices committed by the inhabitants of the village are both made possible and mystified by the use of a specific economic jargon. In the *Threepenny Opera* Macheath is ironically saved, amnestied and even knighted by the Queen at the close of the play, whereas in *Dogville* the ultimate moral agent turns out to be a criminal, playing the role of the Old Testament God. In both texts the surprising finale results in the restoration of an order which is essentially criminal.

In Brecht's play, this criminal order is rooted in the capitalist system, which causes human beings to be morally corrupt and forces them to forget their humanity (Hecht 1985: 215); *Dogville* seems to enact the same criticism (although Grace denies at the end of the film that any social condition or degree of poverty may be considered as an excuse for the amount of injustice committed against her) and the question is whether this is a specific element of von Trier's critique of the United States of America, the 'Land of Opportunities', where he has famously never been.

As the director himself stated during the interview published in this volume, *Dogville*'s basic plot – a stranger enters an established community undermining its moral and social solidity by merely being present – is somehow a dramatic cliché. However, it seems to strikingly resonate in this specific case with the global political situation at the time when the film was made (*Dogville* came out in 2003), when the US, in the aftermath of the attacks of 2001, almost single-handedly took up the role of police and moral force of the world and concocted an arbitrary and ideologically inflected world chart of good and bad nations and peoples. In Lars von Trier's USA, represented by the microcosms of Dogville and Manderlay, Grace is, as a foreigner, suspect, but it is also the embodiment of the forces exposing the true fabrics of a society which sees itself as essentially good because it upholds the vestiges of morality in the form of cultural activity and learning (Tom), hard labour (all of them), patriotism, and a sense of community values. It is ironic that the lyrics of one of the most beloved patriotic songs, 'America the Beautiful', sung in the film at the moment when Grace's status mutates drastically within the community, praises God for shedding 'Grace' on America, which welcomes it in brotherhood. In the film, 'brotherhood' is divested of any positive meaning, like culture, patriotism, communal and democratic values, and becomes just another tool for exercising power, manipulation and prevarication at the expenses of the 'threatening' foreign element. The foreign element (Grace and the mob which are her family) turns out to be part of the very same society which makes Dogville the place that it is – yet only Dogvillians are unable to grasp this fact because they cannot see beyond the petty affairs and interests of their small community. The righteousness of Dogville's inhabitants is exposed as flawed, but the finale also seems to be a critique of the way in which justice is done in the name of a pseudo-religious morality[7] which is ultimately emptied of meaning and put at the service of sheer vengeance and further prevarication – as if violence was inescapably at the roots of such righteous behaviour.[8] In this sense, *Dogville* may be seen as a denunciation of the arrogance and hypocrisy of self-appointed judges of the evils of the world which see themselves as the arm of God on earth. In fact, it could be argued that the projection of a series of photographs of the desperately poor during the credit sequence at the end of the film is intended to stress the hypocrisy of such values as those of community, patriotism and brotherhood in the face of the problems which affect the very core of the nation which is supposed to uphold such moral standards.[9]

The story of *Dogville* and the moral questions it opens up strikingly echo one of the most intriguing plays of contemporary German-speaking literature, Friedrich Dürrenmatt's *Der Besuch der alten Dame* ('The Visit of the Old Lady', 1956). In the Swiss author's play, Claire Zachanassian, an old and eccentric millionaire, and her ninth husband pay a visit to Güllen, her native village in the Swiss mountains which, in spite of the wealth of the rest of the country, is utterly impoverished and forsaken. The once prosperous industry has closed down for unspecified reasons, the train station is almost unused since trains hardly ever stop there, and the population lives in a sort of apathetic and devastating poverty. Claire Zachanassian brings hope to the village with her announcement that she wants to bestow an immense pecuniary gift to the community and to single individuals, on the condition that Alfred Ill, the lover of her youth and now an old man, is killed by one of the citizens. Claire, we slowly begin to understand, had been driven out of the village after getting pregnant and being abandoned by Ill, who paid two witnesses to testify in court that they had sex with Claire instead of him. In that way, Ill could get rid of a cumbersome obstacle to his plan of marrying the daughter of the local milliner and inherit his shop. Claire has come to Güllen to 'buy justice', and her act causes the fragile moral and social fabric of the community to crumble, exposing the hypocrisy of a group of people which, taken one by one, would never hurt anybody, but somehow feel entitled, in the name of a self-fabricated moral standpoint, to actually speculate and make debts on the assumption that indeed somebody will kill Alfred Ill, because that is the right thing to do.

In Güllen, as in the forsaken town of Dogville, poverty rules in the 'Land of Opportunities' and, perhaps for this reason, everybody is ready to play the hangman. In both cases, a glamorous and mysterious woman comes offering a gift, albeit of a very different nature and of a different moral order, and the acceptance of the gift unleashes the destructive powers of a corrupt morality. Again, in both cases, the female protagonist is constructed as a projection surface – from a literary point of view, both Grace and Claire Zanachassian may be seen as allegorical figures, and they sometimes seem to be reduced to mere narrative functions. Claire is a figure who lives in the past, like most of the inhabitants of Güllen – her present is just another rewriting of the past; her actions are not real actions but just mere acts initiating a process of gradual devastation – her agency being that of a mere plot device in a script. As Luigi Forte has noted, she also embodies the threadbare Hollywood clichés about female millionaires or heiresses turned awry – eccentric to the point of grotesqueness, constantly engrossed in their own power, accompanied by a host of shady or clownesque figures, consciously and happily immoral and destructive (Forte 1989: v).

Although Grace does not quite fit these stereotypes, her figure (and the choice of Nicole Kidman as the impersonating actress) consciously refers to the numerous versions of the 'gangster's doll' in literature and especially in classic Hollywood gangster movies – figures characterised by seductive fragility, but often turning out to be unexpectedly cruel and cunning. As a genre, however, the *film noir* is woven into the fabric of *Dogville* through the presence of Lauren Bacall, who is here a mere shopkeeper; in fact, as one reviewer has perceptively noted,[10] the most important American film genres are cited here through the composition of the cast: the Mafia films are represented by James Caan, who also played in *The Godfather I* and *II*, the American independent cinema of the 1970s by Ben Gazzara, who, apart from having played in a number of Italian productions of sometimes dubious quality, has also featured in two films by John Cassavetes (*Opening Night* and *Death of a Chinese Bookie*), the arthouse cinema of the 1990s by Chloé Sevigny (*The Last Days of Disco, Boys Don't Cry, Julien Donkey-Boy*) and Jeremy Davies who also starred in Wim Wenders' *Million Dollar Hotel*. According to the reviewer just mentioned, however, the most significant take on Hollywood cinema is the way in which von Trier dismantles the aura of stardom and aloofness associated with Nicole Kidman, here forced to act in very challenging conditions. Thus, *Dogville* is both a homage to Hollywood and also a hubristic act of re-appropriation of the American cinematic tools and protagonists from a European perspective. In this way, it proposes itself also as a rewriting of cinema from the point of view of its financial, as well as its aesthetic and formal aspects: von Trier founded his own production company Zentropa precisely in order to gain independence as an auteur, and his employment of this selection of American actors, together with his apparent renunciation of the most basic of cinematic elements (realistic settings and scenery), seems to suggest a will to completely rethink cinema and its industry.

In this sense and through its dialogue with the texts mentioned above, we may be able to finally think of *Dogville* not simplistically as a critique of the USA as the 'bad guys' of contemporary history, but rather as a reflection on tainted morality and on the negative power of ideology.

NOTES

1 For an analysis of the relationship between Lukács's concept of 'reification' and Marx's definition of 'objectification', see Fenichel Pitkin (1987).

2 This is, of course, a very simplified account of the issue, but it will suffice for the purpose of this chapter.

3 This emerges towards the end of the film when Grace replies to Tom, who is begging her to make love to him, that he can have her body if he wants, like all the others have.

4 I am indebted to Sara Fortuna for this idea.

5 See interview with the director in this volume.

6 Nina Simone covered the song in the 1960s and linked it to the project of a black revolution. Comic-book writer Allan Moore used it also as an inspiration for his *The League of Extraordinary Gentlemen*. See http://en.wikipedia.org/wiki/Pirate_Jenny, last accessed on 15 May 2012. (Warning: parts of this article are unclear and misleading, suggesting that Pirate Jenny and the character Jenny in the play may be the same person.) Ernst Bloch suggests that the revolutionary impact of the song lies in its mixture of kitsch Christian sentimentality, messianic motifs and blasphemy (1985: 78–9) in spite of the fact that Jenny's pietism in fact turns it into an 'advent's song', rather than a revolutionary one.

7 It has been noted by numerous readers that the final shootout and Grace's protection of the dog Moses has a clear theological subtext.

8 There is a strong connection in this sense between *Dogville* and David Cronenberg's *A History of Violence* (2005), in which a typical American provincial family living a peaceful life in a semi-rural setting turns out to be deeply connected and entangled with the Philadelphia mob.

9 Some of these photographs show the urban poor in contemporary America, others have been selected from the series commissioned by the FSA (Farm Security Administration) between 1935 and 1944 to document the life and difficulties of the rural poor. The contemporary photographs are by the celebrated Danish photographer Jacob Holdt.

10 Unsigned review, *Die Zeit*, 23.10.2003, Nr. 44.

WORKS CITED

Anon., *Die Zeit*, 23/10/2003, Nr. 44.

Bloch, E. (1985 [1929]) 'Lied der Seeräuber Jenny', in W. Hecht (ed.) *Brechts 'Dreigroschenoper'*. Frankfurt: Suhrkamp, 76–80.

Brecht, B. (1998 [1928]) *Die Dreigroschenoper*. Frankfurt: Suhrkamp.

Dürrenmatt, F. (1999 [1956]) *Der Besuch der alten Dame: Eine tragische Komödie*. Zürich: Diogenes.

Fenichel Pitkin, H. (1987) 'Rethinking Reification', *Theory and Society*, 16, 2, 263–93.

Forte, L. (1989) 'Nota Introduttiva', in F. Dürrenmatt, *La visita della vecchia signora*. Trans. A. Rendi. Turin: Einaudi, v–xii.

Hecht, W. (1985) 'Die Dreigroschenoper und ihr Urbild', in W. Hecht (ed.) *Brechts Dreigroschenoper*. Frankfurt: Suhrkamp, 201–14.

Lukács, G. (1971 [1968]) 'Reification and the Consciousness of the Proletariat', in G. Lukács, *History and Class Consciousness*. Trans. R. Livingstone. London: Merlin Press, 83–222.

Nussbaum, M. C. (1995) 'Objectification', *Philosophy and Public Affairs*, 24, 4, 249–91.

The Idiot's Tragedy

SERGIO BENVENUTO

In accepting to contribute to this volume on *Dogville*, my aim was to try and link this film with all of Lars von Trier's *oeuvre*. An author's work is never homogeneous, interwoven as it is with various lines, contingencies and goals, so that it is impossible to extract the 'essence' of either a single work or a single author. Yet, in von Trier's films it is possible to grasp a fundamental, pervasive aim of which *Dogville* is an important stage: that is, the aim of creating a radically tragic *real-ist* (but not *realist*, as we shall see) cinema.

1. Idiocy

Amongst von Trier's films, *Idioterne* (*The Idiots*, 1998) impressed me the most. I have wondered whether this may be due to idiosyncratic reasons of my own, which may not necessarily be shared by others, or whether it is because this film offers an explicit key to understanding the Danish director's other films.

The Idiots is the only one amongst von Trier's films which precisely follows the norms laid out in the Dogme 95 manifesto. It narrates the wanderings throughout Denmark of a group of young men and women, who behave, on occasion, as mental retards. Each one of them has his or her own, not necessarily noble, reason for joining the group. Pretending to be a bunch of noisy fools, for instance, sometimes enables them to be thrown out of a restaurant without paying the bill. Stoffer, the group's leader, theorises an ethical project out of what, at first glance, may appear as a simple goal: to draw out the 'inner idiot' hidden within each of us. But Stoffer's provocative mission really reveals its limits when he asks each person in the group to 'play the idiot' not only in anonymous public places, but also in their own homes or work environment. There, however, no one dares to howl like an idiot, with one exception, as we will soon see.

The Idiots is the second film of von Trier's 'Golden Heart' trilogy – the first being *Breaking the Waves* (1996) and the third *Dancer in the Dark* (2000). The 'golden hearts' are all working-class females. Von Trier considers himself the heir of Carl Theodor Dreyer – and it is not by chance that his two favourites amongst Dreyer's films are *La passion de Jeanne d'Arc* (*The Passion of Joan of Arc*) and *Gertrud*. In both these films the protagonists are victimised women: Joan of Arc is the victim of a political conflict in which she is just a pawn, and Gertrud is punished for her lifelong dedication to love.

Two of von Trier's female protagonists from this trilogy meet a terrible death. Bess, the young bride of *Breaking the Waves*, allows herself to be sexually abused and beaten to death by unknown violent men, in the hope of – superstitiously, magically – saving her husband from permanent paralysis. Selma, the young mother of *Dancer in the Dark*, prefers to risk the gallows rather than deprive her son of the money needed to save his sight. Both sacrifice themselves for male figures.[1] What is striking about both characters is their innocent, infantile, slightly stupid air, as though they experienced the world through an imaginary filter – religious in the case of Bess, theatrical and dance-like in the case of Selma. Their values are not suited for a winners' world. Bess, with her silly beret, holds Calvinist 'dialogues' with the Eternal Father, and she herself responds in His name, severely and gruffly. After her death, her doctor friend comments that 'Bess was good' – indeed a good martyr, albeit a bit stupid.

Even though von Trier did not consider himself to have been inspired by Fellini, some of his heroines remind me of the characters interpreted by Giulietta Masina: Gelsomina (the clown of *La strada*) or Cabiria (the slum prostitute of *The Nights of Cabiria*. And von Trier really loves Liliana Cavani's *The Night Porter*, where a female prisoner of a Nazi lager ends up in a sort of sadomasochistic complicity with her jailor, an SS officer.

At the risk of being accused of misogyny, von Trier closely links femininity with a certain idiocy, which makes women the chosen victims of humiliating persecutions. In fact, one might even wonder whether this is a fantasy which haunts him. Apart from the suspicion of a mental handicap, these characters are sometimes also affected by physical handicaps, as, for example, Selma, the 'dancer in the dark', who is nearly blind. Could von Trier's preference for 'stupid female martyrs' be linked to his process of conversion to Catholicism (converging towards his signing of the *Dekalog* with Thomas Vinterberg, which formed the basis of Dogme 95)? Or perhaps as a reaction to his family's rigorous Communist upbringing? I can think of perhaps only one other great filmmaker – Kenji Mizoguchi – whose cinema is as dominated by the painful figures of humiliated and offended women.[2]

2. Karen's pain

This stupidity of the weak and persecuted does not always carry female connotations. In *Direktøren for det hele* (*The Boss of It All*, 2006), Ravn secretly owns a Danish computer company whose employees believe he is just one of them. All company decisions – especially the most abhorrent ones – are attributed to an imaginary boss who resides in America. When Ravn decides to sell the company to a ruthless businessman (which will imply firing all personnel), he hires Kristoffer, a down-on-his-heels actor, to play the part of the big boss, thus handling over to him any responsibility for the sale. These powerless employees – men and women alike – strike a soft note in us, yet even they convey a sort of sweet idiocy. They believe the unlikely lies that Ravn and Kristoffer dish out and allow themselves to be manipulated at will. These underlings – with their fundamental 'golden heart' – are stupidly good like Bess and Selma; they share nothing of the sharpness or humour of Majakovskij or Brecht's proletarian characters, for example.

Not even *The Idiots* escapes this paradigm of the 'stupid, persecuted, female martyr'. Stoffer's group co-opts Karen, a woman encountered in their runabouts, who, with her innocent and sweet air, seems far from the crazy disorder of the group of fake imbeciles. She seemingly enjoys being part of their adventure, yet somehow remains at the margins of the group. When Stoffer asks each one to 'play the idiot' in their own familiar surroundings, Karen returns home like the others. There, we learn that she had recently lost her son, and that her running away from home was a way to express her pain. It was during her aimless wandering that she met up with this group of 'idiots'. Just a few shots suffice to grasp the grim, desperate climate at her home with icy relatives who despise her. And right in the middle of the family supper, wrapped in bitter silence, Karen indeed plays the idiot. I find this 'Karen returns home' sequence one of contemporary cinema's most touching moments.

It is Karen's courage which in retrospect provides us with a key to reading the entire film. Our timid 'middle-class' Karen is the 'golden heart' *par excellence*: she need not try to draw out the inner idiot, because her pain has already rendered her one. It is precisely because Stoffer's philosophy is so 'ideological' that it is unconvincing. Why should there be an 'inner idiot' rather than an inner crazy person, pervert or tormentor? One might venture to say that it is because von Trier has a weakness for the mentally challenged. In his TV mini-series *Riget* (*The Kingdom*, 1994, 1997) we see a sort of televised version of the Greek Chorus: two actors affected by Down's Syndrome comment on the unfolding story to communicate the tragic tone of the show to the public. Karen's rebellious act amidst her grim family enables us to grasp that the incomprehensible, inarticulate cries of the idiot are a unique expression of pain and desperation. It is the unbearable side of life which turns us into idiots. Playing the idiot unleashes that scream – which is not a cry for help or relief, but rather an expression of our total inadequacy to life.

3. Mulier sacra

Dogville on the other hand seems to deviate from this theme. Its beautiful protagonist Grace is only in part a persecuted woman: in the end she is able to take revenge and her persecutors – the inhabitants of Dogville

– are all killed. But this 'happy ending' is nevertheless disturbing: how can we rejoice in the fact that so many defenceless, albeit mean, citizens are slaughtered by ferocious gangsters? We are ashamed of our very 'virtuous' feelings of revenge which the very film itself provokes.

With *Dogville* the paradigm of the 'Persecuted Woman' seems less pertinent, also because the star who impersonates Grace – the statuesque Australian beauty Nicole Kidman – certainly does not have the *physique du rôle* of the usual pathetic persecuted woman.[3]

But, with her collection of figurines, the beautiful victim has something innocently infantile about her, and when Vera smashes them one by one to punish and torment her, we sense that Grace's pain is like that of a child. It is precisely the childishness of her pain that is so moving in this scene. Yet, while a certain stupidity floats around Grace, in the end we discover that it was contrived.

Grace's situation – more so than that of the heroines of von Trier's other films – seems to echo Giorgio Agamben's *homo sacer*, a judiciary figure of ancient Rome, who had lost any legal right or protection, whom anyone could kill without incurring any sanction whatsoever; he could not, however, be sacrificed. Agamben sees the *homo sacer* in contemporary societies in anybody without legal status – for example, those interned in Nazi concentration camps, illegal immigrants, victims of certain special laws, etc. In short, those reduced to 'bare life', legal non-entities left with only *zoé*, biological life. Grace – increasingly treated as a mere body which anyone in their little town can abuse at will – becomes a *mulier sacra*.[4]

For von Trier the paradigm of exclusion is the Persecuted Woman/ Prisoner, the *mulier sacra* as a bare body at the mercy of others. Whether it be the body for sheer sexual use (Bess), the body as the solitude and idiocy of pain (Karen), the body as blind motherhood, which dreams itself a dancer (Selma), or the body as humiliated slave (Grace).

4. Handicapped cinema?

Yet, von Trier's cinema is not just essentially *about* the physically or mentally handicapped or idiots, or beings – mostly feminine – reduced to bare life. In some way, it is a cinema which itself wants to be handicapped or even a bit stupid. A cinema in its own way stripped *bare*, in contrast with Hollywood's 'well dressed' layered perfection of special effects, the best actors, and masterful editing which leaves us breathless.

As an alternative to this imposition of a 'perfect' cinema on a global audience, the famous *Dekalog* provocatively exploited imperfection by proposing an *invalid* cinema. With Dogme, the director limits himself via seemingly arbitrary norms. Von Trier pursues good cinema not by taking advantage of all available possibilities, but rather by willfully and 'stupidly' restricting possibilities. Dogme addresses the director's 'vow of chastity'; is there anything sillier today than a vow of chastity? Dogme's directors in fact handicap their work in their attempt to create a naïve and rough cinema – which, precisely for this reason, reveals itself as highly sophisticated. Crime and sanctity, knowledge and naiveté are juxtaposed in the same character, as in von Trier's criminal and saintly cinema, whose ultimate refinement is achieved by means of a contrived awkwardness.

In *The Five Obstructions* (2003), von Trier and Jørgen Leth take up as a starting point the latter's film, *A Perfect Human* (1967) which focuses on a self-proclaimed and self-satisfied *perfect human*. Obviously, for us this figure has an air of idiocy about him. And the five obstructions are essentially five constraints – along the lines of the *Dekalog* – that von Trier imposes on the other director. *The Five Obstructions* can thus be read as a manifesto of poetics: in contrast to the polished American cinema, he tries out a European way characterised by shortcomings and idiocies - because only an imperfect cinema can be a *tragic* cinema. In this way, an underlying uncertainty falls over that idiocy that von Trier holds so dear, to contrast the satisfied imbecility of the 'perfect human in a perfect cinema' with that dissatisfied, bare, cruel cinema which puts on stage imperfect human beings.

This desire to handicap his films led to his use of Automavision in *The Boss of It All*. The director set up several movie cameras, but allowed the computer to decide which angle to use, leaving the process of filmmaking to risk and chance, a strategy similar to Pollock's action painting and to Cage's music. So that, in the final version of the film there are gaps in the continuity of the film sequences, imbalances, and so forth. In a sense, this is a way of creating a filmic form which is mostly suitable to its content. The shakiness of the film reverberates the shaky small world of business which the film represents. The harshness of the form alerts us to the harshness of the object. Certain films are irritating because they film misery and degradation but in a polished, slick style which lacks the horror, so that poverty and pain, sublimated by art, seem redeemed. But they are not redeemed in the real world. Instead, through his often artificial and stylised cinema, von Trier wants to *lead us to the Real* – to a bare truth that can only be expressed through idiocy or subjection, and to the cruel crudeness of social relationships.

5. 'Realism' and Real-ism

In so far as it is a self-limitation of expressive possibilities, the *Dekalog* is really just like a game. A game between persons or teams is possible if both accept certain rules, which always imply certain exclusions, that is, that certain plays are unacceptable (for example, a basic rule of football is that no player – except the goalkeeper – can touch the ball with his hands). Today, instead, the idea has taken hold that the artist need no longer be limited by rules or conventions: anything can be utilised to create effects. Contemporary artists produce *installations* which utilise any expressive means, from videos to smells. The *Dekalog* takes the opposite direction with respect to this current promiscuous trend: it aims at re-establishing a certain 'chastity', certain unjustified rules to be obeyed. One could argue that a film is not a team game, but rather a product that should satisfy, above all, the public. But Dogme 95 is a self-imposition of rules concerning moviemakers, not the public. It is the artist's attempt to deprive himself of expressive possibilities, to 'obstruct' himself.

Yet the *Dekalog's* commandments are not completely arbitrary, and seemingly aim to reduce the distance between the cinema of fiction and documentary. However, this reduction of manipulative liberty does not lead to *Vérisme* (to the closest resemblance, the illusionist non-distinction between fiction and reality) but rather to *Real-ism*: towards the Real. I will not enter into details here about all the theories that distinguish reality from the Real. It suffices here to say that the so-called *vériste* cinema tends to give the sensation that we are not watching a film – hence, something artificial or constructed – but rather concrete, real events.Von Trier's Real-ism – not in the least contradictory to Brechtian techniques of estrange-ment – consists rather in making us feel the Real not as something which takes the place of fiction itself, but that toward which the work *tends*.The aim of the *Dekalog*'s self-limitations is not to circumvent the reality in which the filmmaker is working, but to force him in some way to show the existence of this reality *beyond representation*. In von Trier's films, we sense that he is constrained, even if we do not *see* this constraint.

The fourth commandment, '*The film must be in colour*', proclaims the opposite of the formalist and anti-realist idea of cinema, for which true cinema should be filmed in black and white (as Rudolf Arnheim thought) in opposition to the colours present in reality.Yet von Trier's need is not to simulate reality, but to diminish the distance from the real, and the real is coloured.

Take for example the commandment '*Sound must never be produced apart from the images and vice versa*'.This apparently corresponds to a 'realist' need in an illusionist sense: when movie sequences are accompanied by a musical comment, everyone grasps that that music is *external* to the situa-tion and story being recounted.Von Trier would have accepted Coppola's use of Wagner in the scene from *Apocalypse Now* where the captain of a helicopter unit sends all his men off to battle the Vietcong to the sound of the passage from the Valkyrie Cavalcade diffused in every helicopter. The film's character himself uses this musical score in an attempt to turn the experience of war into a Wagnerian opera, to transform the horror and squalor of reality (a cruel war) into a sublime cinematic representa-tion. But it is precisely by denouncing this virtualisation of reality that the Real – that is, what art refers to without representing It – peeks out in this film.This Real is not what is rendered fascinating and gripping by cinema, but what cinema misses, what transcends cinema and what the latter never represents.

Certainly von Trier has not always respected his self-imposed restric-tions. But his entire *oeuvre* carries forward the ethical and aesthetic proj-ect – in opposition to every form of surrealism – of the aforementioned Real-ism. Take the fact that the characters in *Dancer in the Dark* often dance. Dance tends to aesthetically transfigure our lives, so that 'to live as though one were dancing' could be a metaphor for a happy existence.[5] But in this film the dancing episodes are out of sync and in contrast with the misery of Selma, who will never be able to dance – being nearly blind and about to be imprisoned and executed. The choice of the anti-realist form of dance is not resolved in an aesthetic sublimation of a tragic life, but on the contrary, points to real life in all its tragedy. The Real that interests von Trier is that which his false idiots evoke even if only elliptically: the pain and suffering of human existence, in themselves inexpressible and not prettified.

6. To die dancing

Many find in von Trier's films above all another take on Brecht's epic principles. Von Trier would follow up on Godard's cinema, imbued as it was with a Brechtian 'estrangement effect' (*Verfremdungseffekt*). *Breaking the Waves*, *Dogville* and the more recent *Antichrist* (2009) are broken up by actual written chapter headings, with brief summaries, as in old novels. Godard himself recommended reintroducing chapter headings in films. In filming *Breaking the Waves* von Trier was probably thinking back to Godard's *Vivre sa vie: Film en douze tableaux* (*To Live her Life: A Film in Twelve Scenes*, 1962), also about a female prostitute who identifies with Dreyer's Joan of Arc being tried (what a coincidence!), and ends up being killed.

Even Quentin Tarantino uses chapter headings to make his plots progress (as, for example, in *Inglorious Basterds*, 2009). And clearly even here this and other distancing techniques do not diminish in the least the effects of suspense and public involvement. In fact, they accentuate a sort of clinical coldness that does not pertain solely to the film's 'bad guys' (the Nazis in this case) but to the film itself, which unfolds as if it were a duel between the pity of the audience and the ironic indifference of the persecutor.

While on the one hand von Trier may divide a film into chapters, on the other he may make it part of a trilogy. His first trilogy, 'Europe', was followed by the 'Golden Heart' trilogy, and then 'USA: Land of Opportunities'. Even the television mini-series *The Kingdom* was planned as a trilogy. Might his preference for the number three be an attempt to break up the dramatic, inseparable whole of the film into a complete continuum such as we see today: each of his films is divided into small sections, with each film appearing as a fragment of a longer series, like a soap opera. I am convinced that von Trier would approve of the way films are shown in Italy, with an intermission which allows moviegoers to go to the bathroom, buy an ice cream, get a drink, and so forth. To cut and paste – and *show* the cutting or pasting – is a distancing practice.

Dogville and *Manderlay* (2005), in particular, are presented as theatrical stages: instead of houses and streets there are lines and signs on the pavement. Here, von Trier is probably leaning towards the theatrical style of Thornton Wilder's *Our Town* (1938) – a classic example of the indulgence with which the theatre represented the boring, easygoing life of American small towns. Wilder had also reduced to a minimum the staging and its props, but von Trier's infernal 'small town' presents just the opposite of the essentially good and monotonous rhythm of Wilder's town.

The lack of houses and walls in *Dogville* somehow makes its inhabitants visible at every moment. The entire community thus becomes the visible, pervasive protagonist of the film. Individual differences are minimised with respect to the *polis*, united in its shared vileness. And when Grace becomes the slave of that community, we feel even more strongly her imprisonment in a space where everything can be seen by everyone.

However, von Trier does not replicate Brecht's epic theatre: in reality, he opens us up to an extremely *tragic* dimension. Or, one might say, he exalts to the maximum our feelings of *pity* and *anguish* – of *eleos* and *phobos*, to quote Aristotle.

We said that *Dancer in the Dark* presents itself as a film-ballet, but to all appearances nothing could be more estranging. How can one 'identify' with characters who every so often burst into dance? (Who was it that said he didn't like opera because the protagonist keeps on singing at the top of her voice while dying?) And yet, as the story proceeds towards the final catastrophe, our perplexity and shock at this increasingly incongruous dancing grows. The culmination is reached in the atrocious final scenes in which Selma – whom we know is fundamentally innocent – is brought to the gallows. It is painful to see everyone in the grey, gloomy prison, where the execution will take place, start to dance. Dance, always the prototype of pure joy, is scandalously juxtaposed with one of the darkest imaginable situations. Far from estranging us emotionally from Selma's sad destiny, the non-realistic tenor of the film – a dance – heightens our bewilderment.

Thus, von Trier lays bare the 'idiotic' face in all of us, our quasi-stupid innocence, our handicapped side – the other face of our social identity. He attempts to peer into the world of the unhappy, into the reality of social relations which are at once *detached* and *pitiable*.

7. Identifying with one's torturer

In short, von Trier grasped that the Brechtian rhetoric of estrangement, as an ironic detachment from the drama, can be utilised instead to exasperate our affections and pervert our empathies.

Take, for example, Michael Haneke's film *Funny Games* (both versions, 1998 and 2008). Two young angel-faced men dressed completely in tennis whites take an entire family (father, mother and child) prisoner in their country house, and, for pure fun, force on them sophisticated games of torture, to then slowly kill them off one by one in a phlegmatic way. But every so often, in the midst of such cruelty, scenes pop out which 'distance' us from the events. For instance, more than once, one of our handsome torturers turns to the audience and with a wink in his eye, comments on both the public and the film; or, as in another example, when the wife manages to shoot one of the two torturers, the other sadistic angel 'corrects' the scene, rewinding the film so as to make it continue in the 'right' way. *It is scripted* that these defenceless victims will be killed, while the two torturers will get away with it and happily continue their *funny games* with other victims. These distancing expedients, far from easing our involvement, instead increase our anguish and disgust at people being tortured to death. By interspersing moments of meta-communication about the film itself, the director places us squarely in the detached position of the two amused assassins. Not only does the audience mourn for the victims with whom they identify, but the meta-linguistic irony almost forces them to come to identify with the murderers themselves. Haneke thus reveals to us the far from 'fraternal' and fundamentally sadistic presupposition of

Brechtian distancing. An uninvolved glance into suffering and injustice enables us to identify with Brecht's 'oppressors' as much as with Haneke's torturers, who seem to contemplate with distance the misery and pain wrought by them. And, of course, this form of identification disgusts us… Distance can multiply emotions (and not only negative ones).

Pasolini had already suggested this in the final scenes of *Salò, o le 120 giornate di Sodoma* (*Salò or the 120 Days of Sodom*, 1975). In a courtyard, Fascist officials impose horrible tortures upon their young prisoners before killing them. But these scenes are viewed from afar and without sound by the spectator; that is, from the point of view of one of the sadists. In turn, in fact, one of the torturers is seen to observe this cruel scene from a window through opera glasses. But at a certain point, the binoculars are turned around and the cruel events are viewed from an enormous distance. In short, true sadism, more than inflicting pain, consists in considering it from a Brechtian distance – with negative empathy. And our identification with an indifferent estrangement maximises our horror.

In von Trier's films, emotive effects are not entrusted solely to a stylised distancing, but also to 'expressionist' contrivances. For example, for about the first twenty minutes of *Dancer in the Dark*, I experienced an intense, almost physical discomfort. The characters were filmed from too low an angle, leaving no space over their heads. They appear crushed by an imaginary ceiling, like creatures metaphorically caged in misery and illness. But it is precisely this sociological compression that is not merely represented, but *expressed* through a framing style which crushes us.

Brecht's project was ambiguous. This perhaps was precisely why the era in which Brecht found his greatest popularity – the 1960s and 1970s – was also an era where its opposite shone, the Artaud-inspired 'theatre of cruelty'. The avant-garde theatre and cinema of that time was appreciated by both Brechtians and Artaudians. On the one hand, the rational *epic theater* aimed to make us think rather than feel; on the other, the irrational *theatre of cruelty* aimed to upset us. How was it possible to combine Brecht's reflective human detachment with Artaud's inhuman Dionysianism?

In the end, true cruelty – what Sade brings into play – always implies the representation of some distancing, and a certain distancing of representation. Brechtian *Verfremdung* was basically an illusion, in so far as it deceived us about our 'critical' capacities, wanting to lead us to believe that at the theatre we could be 'scientific', leaving us no choice but to identify with our heroes. Von Trier understood that in order to represent the cruelty surrounding the subordinate, female condition on stage, he needed to bring about a distancing, an artificiality which alone is capable of really breaking our hearts.

So what von Trier offers us is an example of radical tragic cinema. In effect, he shows us beings who can do nothing but elicit our pity and anguish. It is precisely because we distance ourselves from the atrocious destinies of Bess, Karen, Selma, Grace, the female protagonist of *Antichrist*, that their stories tear us apart. Many of von Trier's films have a very strong emotional impact, at times going beyond all limits of tolerance. Various people have told me that they were so disturbed by von Trier's films that they no longer go to see them… 'I'm not such a masochist!' Von Trier does not spare the spectator, unlike today's dominant cinema where a happy ending is always obligatory, even if at times disguised as a sad finale. Even Aristotle pointed out that tragedy should not be too bitter, because recounting the story of a truly good man who suffers an absolutely doomed destiny is unbearable, as it wounds the spectator's *philanthropia*.[6] This is why, for example, directors for centuries have refused to allow Cordelia to die at the end of *King Lear*. The audience would never have tolerated it. So, von Trier is attempting a *non-philanthropic*, part-Aristotelian tragedy which does not look towards Hope, but stops short at representing the pain of a life laid bare.

8. Demons in paradise

Von Trier lives in a country which, according to statistics on World Happiness, enjoys the highest levels of social well-being: Denmark. Together with some other Scandinavian countries, Denmark holds first place in the world for quality of life, income per capita, democratic freedoms, social services, environmental sensitivity, life expectancy, etc. Certainly, a country's good fortune is always relative, only when compared with others. Nevertheless, Denmark seems like a happy corner of the planet. Is it a paradox or a symptom that such a tragic cinema has emerged from such an enviable country?

Von Trier often situates his stories of passion and sacrifice in a conformist, cynical, egoistic and slave-driven America – to use certain clichés – in order to give some kind of sociological credibility to his characters' malaise (although he himself has never been in the United States, due to his phobia of flying). The title for his trilogy – 'USA: Land of Opportunities' – has an evidently ironic tone.

The way in which von Trier represents America reminds us of how Brecht evoked Nazi Germany in *Furcht und Elend des dritten Reiches* (*Fear and Misery of the Third Reich*, 1938). Brecht's mosaic-like drama is often performed today, but what is most fundamentally disturbing is not the representation of the degradation of life in a specific totalitarian regime. Rather, Brecht in fact showed us the infernal quality of social co-existence as such, behind the screen of Hitler's terror, as though the Third Reich had brought to light the malice and cruelty intrinsic to human relations. Every country, however good its political system, needs heroes. It is not by chance that some years later, in *Huis Clos* (*No Exit*, 1944), Sartre will finally let one of his characters utter, in a gnomic way, 'hell is other people' – a maxim which could be transformed into 'Nazism is in others'. In von Trier's films, behind the irony of the 'land of opportunities', the way is cleared for an outright denunciation of social life.

In effect, unlike much of leftist cinema or theatre, von Trier does not indulge in any eulogy whatsoever on the fundamental goodness and wisdom of People. On the contrary, *Dogville* shows how 'simple folk' can turn into persecuting monsters. Put any well-meaning person in the right circumstance and he can be transformed into a torturer (as Stanley Milgram showed with his famous experiment[7]). This denunciation of the horror of the banality of everyday life is part of the American tradition. But Dogville, a rogue town, could be located in any part of the world, and it is not by chance that he presents it as a stage city purely made up of signs.

Still, at the end of the film, we see a series of photographs of actual poor Americans in the 1930s, photos which, however, should not be interpreted as a second thought about the theatrical style of the film, as though to say 'look at how the characters in *Dogville* could really have existed in the real America!' What those final photos actually produce is stylistic disorientation. The film in the end resembles a sort of eighteenth-century, quasi-philosophical apology, and, like certain Marivaux dramas (*La dispute*, 1744, for example) that illustrated a scientific controversy, it appears more like a staged parable. The photographs thrust us into the reality of the Depression Era. Just the opposite of what happened in *Breaking the Waves*, where unrealistic graphics interrupted the realistic continuum of the film. Even here, although with the opposite procedure, the director inflicts a screeching style upon us. In *Breaking the Waves* artifice breaks up a likely story situated in a precise time and place, while in *Dogville*, the realism of the final photos breaks up the didactic artificiality of the film.

Von Trier's real intent is, in short, to *dislocate us*. By engrossing us in a situation which seems real, he reminds us that we are dealing only with an artistic fiction; and when we are convinced that we are participating in an almost abstract demonstrative parable, he reminds us that all of this could be true and concrete. This dislocation thus aims at alerting us to the fact that the function of cinema should not be to imitate reality – thus pushing reality more and more to imitate cinema – but to bring us closer to the Real, towards the pain of life laid bare, which cinema can only allude to.

NOTES

1   Some have complained that many of von Trier's scripts are tearjerkers. Indeed, von Trier loves to show us the sad end of, above all, women, as in numerous classic melodramas such as *La traviata* and *Madame Butterfly*.

2   To my mind, Mizoguchi's *The Life of Oharu* (1952) most closely relates to the 'Golden Heart' trilogy in its narration of the pained and sorrowful life of a woman who bears every imaginable kind of wrong, to then end up a poor prostitute.

3   Even Emily Watson, the Bess of *Breaking the Waves*, is somehow too pretty and bright for the part.

4   We might ask why this completely harmless figure of the outsider with no legal rights is so attractive to numerous philosophers and political thinkers today, and

also to some movie directors. It is probably an antiphrastic effect of globalisation: when cultures and economies mix freely, people are impressed by cases which, by contrast, show exclusion.

5 The idea of representing reality as a ballet was taken up, for example, by Paolo Virzì in *Tutta la vita davanti* (2008; 'All of Life Before You'), along the lines of an Italian comedy. At the start of the film, the unemployed protagonist observes the morning crowds as they head to work as though they were dancing. Even here, the choreographic form brings forth an ironic effect, given that the morning commute is usually one of the bleakest moments of the day. The point is that with Virzì it is clearly enunciated that this 'universal ballet' is a subjective perception of the protagonist. In short, 'truth' is reaffirmed via its almost hallucinatory transgression. The tragedy of *Dancer in the Dark* derives instead from the fact that, from being Selma's subjective perception or desire, dance as a form of perception becomes the actual way of being of the film, as if the director had fully taken on the perception of the protagonist. *Verism* in short is undermined by Real-ism.

6 *Poetics*, XIII, 2, 12.

7 Through his experiment, Stanley Milgram in the 1960s demonstrated that the majority of a sample of people, randomly chosen, effectively agrees to torturing another person without opposing any resistance, in a situation in which an authority orders them to do so for supposedly scientific reasons.

WORKS CITED

Agamben, G. (1998 [1995]) *Homo Sacer: Sovereign Power and Bare Life*. Trans. D. Heller-Roazen. Stanford: Stanford University Press.

Brecht, B. (1990 [1938]) *Fear and Misery of the Third Reich*. London: Methuen.

Marivaux, P. C. de Chamblain de (1973 [1744]) *La dispute*, in *Oeuvres Complètes*. Paris: Crémille.

Milgram S. (1983) *Obedience to Authority: An Experimental View*. New York: HarperCollins.

Sartre, J.-P. (1989 [1944]) *No Exit, and Three Other Plays*. Trans. I. Abel. New York: Vintage.

Wilder, T. (2003 [1938]) *Our Town*. New York: Harper Collins.

Dogville,
or the Arrogance of Grace:
Notes on Cinema as Theatre

BRUNELLA ANTOMARINI

So, when consciousness has, as we might say, passed through an infinity, grace will return; so that grace will be most purely present in the human frame that has either no consciousness or an infinite amount of it, which is to say either in a marionette, or in a god (Kleist, *The Puppet Theatre*)

Furthermore I swear as a director to refrain from personal taste! I am no longer an artist. I swear to refrain from creating a 'work', as I regard the instant as more important than the whole. My supreme goal is to force the truth out of my characters and settings. (From the Dogme 95 manifesto)

The film is limited to a closed space in which almost nothing is left of the 'real' world. It looks like a theatre at the time of rehearsal, where actors move in rooms and streets drawn on the ground. The film set is extremely minimal to enable the actors to perform their parts, to remember them. Here the credo of Dogme, aimed at reducing technical devices in order to render 'reality' as natural as possible, is brought to its ultimate consequences, and paradoxically results in a highly artificial landscape where the reduction is far from being realistic.

What is the sense of a theatrical scene within the theoretical programme of Dogme? It seems to envisage a context in which the maximum of realism must be given by a minimum of 'real', 'obvious' or 'natural' environment. The concern of this chapter will be to provide a possible answer to that question.

On a structural level the monothematic set of the town resembles a theatrical stage, deprived of the fourth wall, as well of the walls inside the film set. The camera and the spectators enter the stage, they are 'inside' the stage and take part in the life of the characters/actors. The filmmaker's ability to include the spectator in the most intimate, delicate or even obscene or disgusting events in the life of a small town is rendered here through a paradox: we are included in the 'real' life of a 'theatre'. Why?

On a formal level, the device of the theatrical town where there are no real walls or houses and we imagine seeing 'through' virtual walls allows the plot to be performed on multiple synchronic scenes. This stratagem also allows the actors to act and at the same time to pretend to act: they are invited to be conscious of the fiction or, in other words, they pretend to pretend. The spectator's voyeuristic eye is satisfied, and simultaneously the actor's self-consciousness is enhanced. We (as spectators) seem to witness a rehearsal in which the illusion is not perfect, as if we expected the film to take place somewhere else, or some other time. Actors act mechanically, as if their aim were just to remember their parts. They look like puppets.

1. The game

Only one scenario accompanies the whole film: actors and spectators are in a town and on a set, inside and outside of the streets and the buildings. The 'town' is a stage, surrounded by darkness and lit by artificial lights. The separations are given only by lines drawn on the ground. The actors pretend to shut doors and to move imaginary objects. The static scene is moved only by the jump-cuts and quick zooms of the hand-held camera. The resulting motion is meant to convey a sense of active participation, and is counter-balanced by a perpendicular bird's-eye view which some-times overarches the scene. We have the impression of being in a kind of videogame, in which actors are pawns, whose quality of 'puppets' is even clearer. It is mainly the set design that determines the identity of the play-ers, the rules, the solution to disorder, and the final dénouement.

Dogville immediately appears as a mixed-media event, in which the cinema contributes to the intrusive perception of the camera; the theatre to the physical presence and auratic distance; the videogame atmosphere emphasises the puppet-like quality of the characters, who seem to be moved by a hidden force; the division into 'chapters' and a literary and slightly ironic voice-over, describing and explaining events, conveying an impression of narrative fiction as if sense could be delivered *only* as nar-rated. The general effect is sometimes irritating. The emotional distance is alternatively restored and destroyed as if the spectators were invading the stage and then put at a distance that makes them feel powerless when confronted with violence.

In conflating separate scenes in one shot, the camera blurs points of view. It seems as if spectators were exposed to the heterogeneity of the characters' desires. Consequently, we have more than one sequence of events at the same time. Whereas a sequence endows facts with a causal order, the lack of walls and narrative simultaneity recalls a certain auto-poietic organisation of facts and gestures. In that respect, theatrical slow-ness seems to be an aid to the spectator, who is invited to follow more scenes at once.

2. The rule

Dictum ac factum, the motto of the town, is written on a wooden sign, marking Grace's hiding place at the beginning. What is said is imme-diately done: words are rules of behaviours and decisions, and facts are applications of communicated rules. There must be a certain particular rule in town.

Spectators are exposed simultaneously to the description of Dogville and to the illustration of a moral programme, the author of which, the young writer Tom, calls 'moral rearming'.

The town, completely closed within the natural borders of the Rocky Mountains, seems to suffer from the inability to 'receive', that is, to accept a gift. A gift being something that comes from 'outside', from someone who does not owe anything to the recipient: being shut inside a totalising environment, that peculiar community cannot learn how to 'accept' or to 'give', that is, to lose and to modify its identity.

Dogville seems caught in the net of selfishness and pettiness, an inevitable rule governing the behaviour of its citizens. In fact, the lack of walls prevents them from having a personality of their own, undergoing a constant and mutual observation and control, as happens in small social environments. They do not seem to be aware of this and it is 'natural' for them to be deprived of what protects and separates individual identities. Their controlled gestures and utterances have an almost ritual character, never instinctive, rather a matter of learning and being careful to fulfil rules in the proper way.

The reason for such strict control seems to be economic poverty. But there is also a philosopher in the town: Tom. His counter-rule of 'moral rearming' is meant to change this miserable condition governed by material need. In fact there seems to be no other source of social life other than poverty. It is the only system to which the citizens can and must adjust. In a more complex social order, houses serve the purpose of protecting individual lives from the very social system; at home we can invent our own sub-systems, different from the social one, in which we can have friendships, loves and pleasures in their own individual expressions. Here the lack of walls and the piercing eye of the filmmaker/spectator prevent the possibility of those protective sub-systems.

Here is a first answer to my question: the citizens' social life is exclusively led on a stage. The stage guarantees that a certain rule is followed, and that poverty is kept within certain bearable limits. In this lack of counter-social strategies the citizens' lives flow in a kind of slumber. Dialogues are direct and harsh, and the voices are low, meditative or attentively predisposed to act cautiously and consciously. Their voices often have a tonality of confessions. Tom aims to accomplish his programme through public meetings, by means of what he calls 'illustrations'. No one in town participates willingly in Tom's programme, which they consider just another social ritual. Throughout the film a voice-over describes what is going on or anticipates the next event, as an omnipotent narrator, who doesn't seem to refrain from destroying all surprise. What happens is what is written in a script and acted according to rules, as if there were no contingency, as if all circumstances were but pretexts.

Suddenly there comes to town a woman who gives Tom the chance to apply his rule. The game undergoes a shock: the players must change the rule. The citizens have the opportunity to learn how to 'give'. During the film a recursive phrase shows the effect of the change: 'a tiny change in light over Dogville'. The attempt to change a moral condition is shown by light, nothing that involves individual behaviours or attitudes, but a general perception of the dark background. The artificial darkness is said to become an artificial light. The hopelessness of the moral change is expressed by the feebleness of that expression.

3. The player

'You have two weeks', says Tom to Grace. After using Grace, who makes a sudden irruption in town, as the test person for the new rule, Tom realises that she can stay if she gives gifts to the citizens; but the gifts must be useless, that is, the citizens must receive from her what they do not need. The new rule – learning to receive through accepting Grace's gifts – soon reveals its ambiguity: the gift is an exchange; in fact the citizens know they can use Grace's need to stay. And she can play on for two weeks: there is a deadline to her adjusting to the citizens' greedy exploitation of her generosity. But the more they realise the risk they take in keeping Grace in town, the higher the stake and the requests to her.

Is that 'tiny change in light over Dogville' the symptom of an inadmissible revelation? Grace – which means beauty and salvation in the Judeo-Christian tradition – seemingly works as an instrument of atonement, whose agent is Tom's experiment. Grace must win by losing, lending herself to the perverse requests of the citizens who in exchange would learn how to 'receive'. The rule is clear and the way every player follows it is consistent, but for Grace's excessive passivity. Why does she accept the role of the sacrificial victim?

Actually she sees some beauty in the disgusting rule that turns her into a slave. Her confidence in Tom is similar to the confidence believers may have in their religions, however violent or unjust. She yields to the increasingly hard social requests. There is the same kind of naiveté about her, that can be found in other films by von Trier, like *The Idiots, Breaking the Waves* and *Dancer in the Dark*, in which innocent characters are accused of being wrong or guilty, and are unable or do not want to defend themselves, whereas every other player is described as cunning and weak, hypocrite and sneaky – especially the male characters – or utterly aggressive – especially the female characters. The distinction between good and evil appears as indubitable, which should make it easy for Tom to accomplish his pedagogical goal, in which the 'illustration' players represent general ideas anyone can embody.

4. The gift

The 'illustration' of the process occurs by degrees, as may happen in different 'levels' of a videogame. Grace has a deadline to accept the rule and stay. But she must overcome different 'levels' of obstacles:

First level:
Nobody wants Grace's gratitude. It seems to be a form of generosity but it is actually a primitive form of aggression.

Second level:
Everyone in the town ends up by accepting that Grace should return their 'generosity' by agreeing that she perform some 'useless' work, such as weeding, looking after a blind man, or a disabled girl. All this work is described as useless in order to keep her in a state of constant debt.

Third level:
As the risk of keeping her in the town increases, they let Grace do 'useful' or necessary work. But that again is not taken as a gift they receive, but as a favour they do.

Fourth level:
Grace is turned into a slave. She is raped and chained around the neck. The citizens feel she owes them this. She is the designated victim, showing that acts of 'giving' and 'receiving', done for their own sake, do not exist at all. Another rule is needed and will be introduced and followed in order to win the game.

The ambiguity of the gift becomes clearer and clearer as the film proceeds. An offer must be returned, an offer that is not returned creates an embarrassing situation. The altruist receives a power that cannot be accepted; therefore, either the offer must be returned, or the altruist must be declared responsible for some misdeed that turns a good deed into a guilty act. Grace submits to any possible violence in her effort to show that she does not want to have any power over the citizens; she just wants to give without receiving anything in exchange. Since the citizens 'have a problem' with the act of 'receiving', they are unable to recognise Grace's gifts and therefore they victimise her.

The motif of altruism – present also in *Dancer in the Dark* and *Breaking the Waves* – is constantly associated with a victim. The more unselfish the person, the easier the victimisation. The redeemer is assaulted, humiliated or killed. The dynamics of 'giving' for the sake of giving is connected to the 'victim' because, as Réné Girard shows in his scapegoat theory (1977), the one who acts in a way that everyone else should but cannot is envied and later hated and therefore found guilty of something in order to justify the hate. The common hate causes an occasion for the community to unite. The community of Dogville designates the 'stranger' Grace as guilty of bringing disorder among them; they project onto her the threat of social violence that constantly lingers in the air over Dogville. In fact, they have found their scapegoat, the victim giving them a reason to feel a renewed solidarity against a common enemy. They seem to find even some happiness, after Tom has denounced Grace to the police, there is a strange calm over the town while waiting for the police. Paradoxically, happiness itself is a product of hostility, it is evidence that something has happened as an unpredictable by-product of Tom's programme: the self-recognition of the community against a scapegoat.

According to Girard, after 'scapegoating', a community tends to turn its designated victim into a sacred entity, in order to dissimulate the crime. Here we do not have any equivalent event, but surprisingly, we might find a visual equivalent: a painterly representation of Grace as a Renaissance Madonna.

Once more, she undergoes violence as a punishment she deserves for some absurd wrong deed she is supposed to have done. Instead of fleeing in a truck carrying apples, she is raped in it. Repeatedly throughout the film, her body's privacy is violated as if a wall of protection is ignored. She becomes – for spectators only, though not for the community – the suffering divinity. A bird's-eye take reveals her body surrounded by apples making her look like a bi-dimensional painted saint. Only the beauty of art ransoms her violated beauty.

Left: Carlo Crivelli, *Madonna and Child* (1480–86); right: still from *Dogville*

The repetition of exemplary actions underlines their accomplishment of a moral rule and being valuable only as such, rather than for their practical necessity. Grace is unaware of being caught in Tom's programme (or social game). She accepts it, because it is different from the violence that compelled her to hide in Dogville.

But her own offer of herself is immediately turned into a gift she receives. She thinks she is acting out of her freedom to give, while Dogville's citizens think she simply *must* do what she does. The disposition to 'lose' that inheres in the gift, is turned into blackmailing, a way they have to punish the superiority of an act of which they are incapable.

Who is generous here? The transparency of the rule – the hidden rule brought to the surface through the device of the gift – reveals that the generous are the ones who *receive* with generosity; the grateful are the ones who give with guiltiness. Once the walls/barriers are brought down, the transparency reveals the paradoxical reversal of sense and the chiasmic rule of the gift:

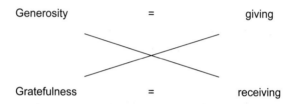

5. Theatre as primeval experience

The rule revealed by the transparency of walls seems to need a theatrical set that betrays the filmic structure. The black background, the artificial light on the stage, the fact that actions are symbolic rather than taken from the 'real world', the voice-over clarifying and sometimes anticipating the next scene, all this contributes to introducing the spectators to a kind of medieval *sacra rappresentazione* (a theatrical representation of the Bible), in which a community actively participates in a religious ritual. In the Middle Ages, theatre and painting were called 'the Bible of the poor', as they were meant to transmit the teachings of the Bible, its moral rules, and to guide behaviours. Actors and audience were close to one another in the square of the town; actors were a real presence representing virtues, vices, or personifications of abstract ideas.

Theatre was then an 'illustration' rather than a more or less plausible narrative.

Tom, defined as a 'writer who does not write', is actually setting up a representation, which he himself calls an 'illustration' of a moral programme. Transmitted on stage, the drama of the Cross could immediately convey the supernatural meaning of the sacrifice turned into resurrection, and the victim turned into a god. Very often actors personified religious values or virtues, like 'Grace'.

This reference, however coincidental, shows that resorting to theatre here is not the betrayal of the Dogme manifesto, but rather the reinforcement of its statement that what is 'real' is theatre. There is nothing outside of it, theatre does not reproduce something external to itself, but it presents, or reveals, the 'real' rule of moral behaviour and the rule of moral behaviour is to pretend to give, while receiving. Human behaviour is governed by the fiction of violence disguised as 'sacred' event.

According to Jean Baudrillard, a simulacrum is 'what bears no relation to any reality whatever: it is its own pure simulacrum' (see 2001: 166–84). But, von Trier could add, this simulacrum is the real engine of human behaviour.

Walls are not only physical protections of biological existences, but symbolic values, hiding and protecting individuals from the inadmissible rule of their behaviour. They are inner distinctions, much more demanding and strict than physical borders. The film has a kind of demonstrative force: once the walls are taken off, the nakedness of individuals in the face of the moral rule governing them comes to light; maybe that is the 'tiny change in light over Dogville'.

The lack of landscape compels the camera to focus on faces and bodies, apart from those few objects left as sign-posts of a real environment, a spaceless place where movements and gestures are slow as if for lack of air. Apparently, this stage is a physical and violent projection of the psyche. Characters are violated and revealed at the same time, until the final fire, which arrives as a natural outcome and a cathartic liberation.

The missing walls reveal the violence of intimacy, or avoid the tenderness of intimacy. In any case, they reveal the 'real "fiction"' that theatre can present, and that the cinema, with its intrinsic illusionism, could not, unless it uses theatre as its object.

Now another question arises: why cinema then, and not real theatre? Because cinema can represent theatre as real, as meta-theatre – the theatre of life, which represents itself. Theatre in a film guarantees the exhibition of the dual character of life: the real as theatrical.

6. Grand Finale: whose victory is it?

As landscape and town are reproduced like a map and the bird's-eye takes reveal the puppet-like character of the game, nothing is left hidden. Just as in a videogame, the player must overcome obstacles and destroy enemies, by following rules and jump to the next level. If Grace is the player surrounded by friends/enemies whom she must cope with, she should increase her powers over time – the greater the obstacles, the stronger the powers. Can the analogy go further? Has Grace super powers? She seems to lose the game, and willingly at that. But her idea that losing (giving) is her force, is challenged and frustrated throughout the whole film.

Yet she is not simply destroyed; she goes on, with her failures, until the last long scene, in which her father (who had been looking for her since the beginning of the film) finds her.

Then something changes... Are we suddenly thrown into another game, must we use another rule? We are suddenly brought back to the cinema, to the visual game of the cinema: the moment of dénouement, an action for action's sake; no more ritualistic slowness, but American quick takes, dialogues, directness of communication, decision-making, and an action movie.

We learn her father's version of her strange behaviour: she is arrogant, he says. During their dialogue in a car – another closed environment, another figure of the unconscious – they keep repeating this word: 'arrogance'. It is the key-term to cause a reversal of the game (and the rule), and a reaction on the part of Grace.

Grace's arrogance consists exactly of giving without taking in return. It is a false morality. It is the inextricable superimposition of good and evil that Grace's arrogance ignores or claims to overcome.

Echoing Nietzsche, Grace's father unmasks the ethical revelation of the film: her innocence had compelled her to flee his arbitrary violence only to embrace an inevitable violence of poverty and need. She felt the pain and the mercy of that. But after so much suffering, her threatening father is actually the only person who shows love to her, and the miserable citizens of Dogville end up by been pawns in Grace's mind. She thought she would welcome them in her infinite goodness, and to be welcomed by them for her infinite goodness. The grace needed to overcome evil is false; it is but a theatrical device. Who is the saviour? It is not Tom with his fake 'moral rearming'; it is not Grace, with her peculiar arrogance; it is not her father, with the arrogance of his violence. After long minutes in which the spectators are left in the dark, in the increasing darkness of the theatre-cinema, Grace orders her father's gangsters to kill every single citizen of Dogville, and their disgusting presence, together with their social or moral rules, is cathartically destroyed. In the final fire, illuminating darkness for the first and last time, all kinds of violence become one and the same. The word 'arrogance' resounds as the arrogance of power, blackmail, vengeance, envy, forgiving, giving, receiving, morality, hidden social laws, strength, and weakness. If just a 'tiny change of light' passes between ethical law and aggression, it takes a total fire to reveal the truth.

It takes a total simulation to express this hyper-realism of a naked inadmissible truth. The player in this piece has been used, exploited and even raped, in order to have access to that truth.

Is it a pessimistic message? Or is it a conditional, relative pessimism, according to which whenever a space is closed in itself, the rule is destruction. Or whenever a space is self-sufficient, a map encompassed in itself and deprived of its distinctions (walls), the rule is destruction. Or whenever we pretend to apply moral laws without any awareness of their hidden real law, the rule is destruction. What protects us from violence (the walls) also protects us from the truth, because the truth is violent; certainly when it is a social truth, grounded on aggression and sacred victimisation.

Why then did it take the device of theatre to exhibit this message? A last tentative answer is that theatre and cinema in this film are mutually and simultaneously analysing themselves in order to reveal the process of unmasking the fake relationship between good and evil. Cinema is a strategy of revelation – perfectly in tune with the Dogme statement – only if it renounces its means, its distinction from another medium, and is mediated by another one. No one is spared in the final purification ritual by fire. Grace's final act does not restore any possible distinction between good and evil, cinema and theatre; she destroys it. It is a hopeful collapsing of walls/barriers.

WORKS CITED

Baudrillard, J. (2001) *Selected Writings.* Ed. M. Poster. Trans. J. Mourrain. Stanford: Stanford University Press.

Girard, R. (1977 [1972]) *Violence and the Sacred.* Trans. P. Gregory. Baltimore: Johns Hopkins University Press.

Bingo!
The Spiritual Automaton in
Lars von Trier's *Dogville*

ASTRID DEUBER-MANKOWSKY

Translated by Katrin Wehling-Giorgi

1. Two kinds of belief

In Lars von Trier's *Dogville*, Tom Edison (Paul Bettany) says 'Bingo!' just before he is shot by Grace (Nicole Kidman), after her experience of being the martyr in the small town of Dogville. Tom's 'Bingo!' refers to the 'clear illustration' that Grace, according to Tom, has given with the transformation of the small town into an inferno, and with the annihilation of all its inhabitants. Just before Grace pulls the trigger he asks for her permission to use this 'clear illustration' as an inspiration in his writing. For Grace, however, the destruction of the town and its inhabitants is not an illustration but a necessity to enable her to restore belief in the world.

Restoring belief in the world, according to Gilles Deleuze, is the necessary task of modern cinema. This belief is, of course, different from Grace's. It does not call for annihilation and vengeance and it is not opposed to thought, but it leads to a state of suspension. For Deleuze, the salient characteristic of modern times – by which he is referring to the post-World War II period – consists in the broken link between man and the world.[1] For this reason cinema, when it stops being bad, 'must film, not the world, but belief in this world' (2005b: 166). The restoration of belief in the world, according to Deleuze, is closely linked to the evocation of a thinking of the unthinkable. He locates this phenomenon in the late films of Danish director Carl Theodor Dreyer, and equally in the films of Rossellini, Godard, Rohmer, Pasolini, Bresson and Antonioni.

Deleuze intends to think with cinema, and thinking with cinema for him means thinking the spiritual automaton, evoked in us by the automatic movement of the cinematic image. In what way does the spiritual automaton emerge in *Dogville*? Does the calculus of von Trier's cinema, which manifests itself in the operationalisation of moral conflicts, as well as in the application of technology according to firm rules, apply to the image or to the thought in the image? (2005b: 168). Is the question of grace or chance, to cite Deleuze, a 'theorematic' or 'problematic' (2005b: 169) deduction? Or should the terminology which Deleuze has created in his philosophy of cinema be applied to films like *Dogville* in the first place?

Von Trier's films cause irritation. They evoke tears, anger, enthusiasm and/or aversion. They are inspired by de Sade's sexual imagery, they are permeated by sexual violence, they stage melodramatic female characters as Christ figures while at the same time are influenced by German expressionist cinema and Dreyer's existentialist films. They play with the notion of miracle, evoke associations relating to sacrificial theology, and are the popular subject of both psychoanalytical interpretation[2] and of the young discipline of 'image' or 'film theology' (see Martig 2008). While its representatives admit that, from an 'aesthetic' point of view, a 'catholically oriented, image-related understanding of identity in terms of the theological notion of "Real Presence"'(Martig 2008: 140) cannot be established in von Trier's films, they do however recognise a 'serious theology of a search for traces' (Martig 2008: 143) in them. If we are to agree with film theorist Gertrud Koch, von Trier's films, irrespective of borrowing from religious motifs, are not religious films. Rather, as she convincingly argues, they are the 'agency of a cinematographic style ... which one last time conjures the power of belief in the aesthetic illusion' (2005). However, in what relationship does this self-reflexive turn of faith to the film aesthetic illusion stand with respect to Deleuze's requirement, according to which the task of modern cinema consists in filming the belief in the world? Which belief and which world is put to the test in *Dogville*? To take the question even further, can von Trier's cinema, or *Dogville*, make us think with cinema in the Deleuzian sense?

2. The spiritual automaton

Deleuze introduces the term 'spiritual automaton' with the designation of the cinematographic image as movement-image (2005b: 251). He departs from the observation that, unlike dramatic or choreographic images, the movement of cinematographic images no longer depends on a moving body and, unlike painting, it does not rely on a spirit which reconstitutes the images in a fictional or mental space (2005b: 151). Deleuze distances himself from the idea that cinema gives us an image which is only set in motion retrospectively. Instead, as Deleuze argues together with the first film theorists such as Sergei Eisenstein, David Wark Griffith, Abel Gance and the representatives of expressionist cinema in Germany, in the cinematographic image, the image 'makes' movement.[3] These thinkers acted on the assumption that the 'simple idea' that cinema as industrial form of art achieves 'self-movement, automatic movement', and that it makes movement the 'immediate given of the image' (ibid.).

Deleuze argues that in the identity of image and movement, the cinematographic image of early cinema actually implemented what remained at the level of request or mere possibility in the other arts. In the execution of movement, the image becomes *perception-image*, an unmediated form of perception (2005a: 66). With the emergence of the movement-image and film, it is the 'world which becomes its own image, and not an image which becomes world' (2005a: 59). With cinema, to quote Raymond Bellour, the 'new beginning of the world takes shape as an ensemble of images' (1999: 51). The automatic movement of the image – which forms the basis of the philosophical pertinence of cinema for Deleuze – replaces the difference between the world and consciousness, as well as the difference between intellect and matter.

The automatic movement of the cinematographic image, as Deleuze summarises, gives rise to 'a *spiritual automaton* in us, which reacts in turn to movement' (2005b: 151). He refers to Leibniz's *Monadology* in this context. By terming the soul a 'spiritual automaton', the philosopher had opposed the dualism of Descartes' *res cogitans* and *res extensa*. Unlike Descartes, who had considered the automaton nothing but a lifeless and mechanical machine by terming the soul a 'spiritual automaton', Leibniz perceives it as a simultaneously simple and animate, self-moving substance. Deleuze adopts the link between soul and movement, but he substitutes the word 'soul' with the terms developed in the context of the 'scientification' of the soul, psyche and brain. Hence he attempts to conceptualise the term 'brain' in particular not as an object but, in line with Alfred North Whitehead's philosophy, as a subject (see Deleuze and Guattari 1991: 211).

For Deleuze, the term 'spiritual automaton' unifies two co-existing and complementary meanings. In the first meaning, the spiritual automaton indicates 'the highest exercise of thought, the way in which thought thinks and itself thinks itself in the fantastic effort of an autonomy' (2005b: 252). In the second meaning, the spiritual automaton denotes a 'psychological automaton who no longer depends on the outside because he is autonomous, but because he is dispossessed of his own thought, and obeys an internal impression which develops solely in visions or rudimentary actions (from the dreamer to the somnambulist, and conversely through the intermediary of hypnosis, suggestion, hallucination, obsession, etc.)' (ibid.). Hence the spiritual automaton combines the counter-striving tendencies of autonomy and independence, or freedom and necessity, without as a matter of fact reconciling or sublating them in a dialectical move.

According to Deleuze, not only are art and philosophy newly united by cinema, but also science, in particular psychology and neuroscience, which is similarly involved in the concrete form assumed by the spiritual automaton under the conditions of cinematography. Deleuze thinks cinema with the term spiritual automaton as an intersection at which the three levels of art, science and philosophy converge. Six years later, in *What is Philosophy*, Deleuze and Félix Guattari likened the intersection of the three levels of art, science and philosophy with the brain become subject ('Thought-brain') (1991: 210). The spiritual automaton, one could summarise, is the form assumed by the precarious 'identity of world and brain' (Deleuze 2005b: 198) in the transforming intersection of art, science and philosophy.

3. Sublime cinema

For von Trier, the theorists of early cinema, as we shall see, are the masters of cinema to which we must return and to whom we must learn from. For Deleuze, the theorists of early cinema, on the other hand, were the creators of a sublime form of cinema and of an art of the masses which have lost their meaning in the aftermath of World War II, National Socialism and Stalin's politics. For the theorists of early cinema, cinema was a 'subjective and collective automaton for automatic movement', as Deleuze shows in particular with the example of Eisenstein's cinematographic theory, but which equally applies to Vertov, Gance, Griffith and German expressionist cinema. As Deleuze summarises, the spiritual automaton was 'the art of the "masses"' (2005b: 152). The films were intended to provide the spirit with the idea of sheer greatness, the idea of an absolute whole (see 2005b: 152–3).

In this predisposition to the sublime, as Deleuze shows with Eisenstein's example, lies the revolutionary force and, as he suggests in reference to Leni Riefensthal's films on the other hand, the unsettling aspect of an art of the masses. 'Worse still', as Deleuze maintains, 'the spiritual automaton was in danger of becoming the dummy of every kind of propaganda' (2005b: 152). In the latter case shock merges with the 'figurative violence of the represented' rather than, as Deleuze implies, 'achieving that other violence of a movement-image developing its vibrations in a moving sequence which embeds itself within us' (ibid.).

Hence, according to Deleuze, we are dealing with two different forces. One of them is manipulative, the violence of the represented, while the other compels to think the whole, the violence of the movement-image and its vibrations. Both assume a strong bond between man and the world, which Deleuze terms the sensory-motor link.

The existence of the sensory-motor link corresponds to a sublime form of cinema, a cinema of mass-art, a revolutionary cinema, an affective action cinema whose wealth derives from the violence of the movement-image. It corresponds to the idea of a physical power of thought that would be placed in a circuit in order to 'deduce his ideas from each other' (2005b: 161). For Deleuze, the idea of the physical power of thought repeats itself in the meaning ascribed to montage and the right continuity shots in sublime cinema. It is a cinema in which everything is based on stimulus and immediate reaction. A cinema in which the nervous vibration leads us, as Deleuze summarises Eisenstein's equation of montage and thought-montage: to 'no longer [be able to] say "I see, I hear", but I FEEL, "totally physiological sensation"' (2005b: 153). The leading idea of thought is here cinematographic in a literal sense. It amounts to the assumption that it is 'the set of harmonics acting on the cortex which gives rise to thought', to, as Deleuze adds, a 'cinematographic I THINK'. The whole appears as subject and the subject as whole.

4. The mummy

In sublime cinema, thought's power of thinking the whole is not questioned but evoked. Sublime cinema's tendency towards totality, as Deleuze shows in a paradoxical turn, leads to thinkers such as Antonin Artaud losing their belief in cinema. In a text written in 1933, Artaud defames the image world of abstract-experimental cinema and of commercially-figurative Hollywood, the power of aesthetic illusion as 'the imbecile world of images caught as if by glue in millions of retinas'.[4]

The experience of the sublime is according to Deleuze replaced by the experience of the movement-image that has superseded one's own thoughts. An abyss emerges between the thought evoked by the movement-image and one's own thought. Deleuze, however, does not consequently infer a critique of cinema, but he interprets the impotence of thought which has been made obvious by Artaud as an experience which thought has within itself. He turns the crisis which cinema entered as a mass automaton with fascism, National Socialism and Hollywood's commercially-figurative cinema into a crisis which concerns thought itself.

From now on a transformed cinema – the cinema which, as Deleuze restrictively phrases it, constitutes the 'soul of cinema' (2005b: 210)[5] – will no longer prove the power of thought but, on the contrary, its impotence.[6] Cinema still involves neurophysiological vibrations and it still relates to the 'inner reality of the brain', only that this inner reality is no longer a whole but, as Deleuze affirms together with Artaud, a rupture or a break. No longer does the whole appear on the screen, but the void or the distance, the deferral between stimulus and reaction.[7] The cinema of the movement-image has become the cinema of the time-image.

Deleuze locates the first realisation of this kind of cinema in the films of Italian Neorealism. 'It is here that situations', as he summarises, 'no longer extend into action or reaction in accordance with the requirements of the movement-image.' We are merely dealing with 'pure optical and sound situations, in which the character does not know how to respond' (2005b: 261). People have lost the belief in their perceptions, and this belief is meant to be restored by cinema (2005b: 166).

The cinematographic insight of the time-image is that the ability to think cannot be forcefully achieved but it requires a choice, or rather a leap. With the examples of Dreyer's late films, *Ordet* (1955) and *Gertrud* (1964), Deleuze shows that ultimately it all amounts to the choice of choice. In what follows I will go into some further detail concerning Deleuze's interpretation of these films, which are also of fundamental significance for von Trier's understanding of cinema; von Trier's view of these films is, however, very different from Deleuze's.

As Deleuze argues in a bold, almost vertiginous interpretation of *Ordet*'s closing scene, the spiritual automaton in Dreyer's film has transformed into a 'mummy'. In order to understand this allegation, one first of all has to follow Deleuze's argument that the spiritual automaton in modern cinema is no longer a mass-automaton. Rather, the spiritual automaton now describes the psychic situation of a seer who sees better and further the less he can react, that is, according to Deleuze, the less he can think what he sees. The seer sees but is unable to relate to what he sees, he cannot think it. But what does the seer see? It is something unbearable: it is the transfixed thought which has eluded him, the thought to which any connection has been truncated and by which he is simultaneously haunted. In the transfixion of thought, the spiritual automaton has turned into a lifeless mummy.

The scene which von Trier adopts, cites and perverts into a rape scene in *Dogville* is set in a room which is open to onlookers. In *Ordet* the daughter-in-law, sister-in-law, mother and beloved wife, Inger (Brigitte Federspiel), is laid out in an open coffin. The corpse is surrounded by father-in-law, brother-in-law, her husband, the doctor and the priest. She lies in a coffin covered in white silk, the light shines through the windows covered with white curtains which filter the light and appear to cover the whole scene with a veil. The camera is in front of the coffin, the dead woman and her beaming white dress, while her folded hands and her immobile young face are seen transversely from above. From here the camera slowly moves towards the living, who for their part look like automata, it moves at knee-height with them around the coffin and only comes to a halt once the first words are uttered. There is a clock on the wall, a lifeless automaton itself, a mummy with an immobile pendulum. For Deleuze, the 'young, dead, cataleptic woman' (2005b: 165) lying in her coffin is the image of thought turned into a mummy.

Since the beautiful, corpse-like body is likened to thought with which every link has been abandoned, the awakening of the dead appears as a resumption of the link between thought and life at the same time. Deleuze accordingly interprets the brave deed of Johannes, the second eldest son who has lost his mind studying Kierkegaard and rediscovered it through Inger's (apparent) death, philosophically and from a Nietzschean perspective as an affirmation of life. Johannes awakens Inger to life through his belief, which Deleuze interprets as the belief in life. According to Deleuze, he re-establishes the link between thought and 'unthought', between thought and life. To the family, as Deleuze writes, he restores 'life and love, precisely because he has ceased to be mad, that is, to believe *himself* to be in another world, and because he now knows what believing means' (2005b: 165). Once the (seemingly) dead Inger has obeyed Johannes's word and has woken up, the pendulum has been newly activated and time can start afresh.

Belief for Deleuze means to tie the bond between thought and life. Belief is a different expression for the affirmation of life. For Deleuze, this does not represent an alternative to thought, but it demands a stricter or more profound thought which lies beyond all certitude of belief.

5. Lars von Trier: religion on screen

Von Trier is well known not only for his films, but equally for his self-dramatisation, his pleasure for provocation and the obsession with the topics of manipulation and control. His films both form part and are the product of a related system of rules at the centre of which stands the myth of the filmmaker as creator. These often provoking sets of rules – which frequently involve psycho-games – are communicated by von Trier through planned public appearances, interviews, the publication of diaries, through trailers or in the end credits, on the Internet or as 'Added Value' in the DVD editions of the films. Von Trier is not only a director but also an entrepreneur who has built up a small media universe with his independent production company, Zentropa, which was founded in 1992, and which produces films for cinema, television films and series as well as commercials. He thereby caters to the demands and economic rules of the neoliberal arts market whilst at the same time playing with them. Zentropa has become well-known mainly due to the Dogme 95 Manifesto and the Vow of Chastity, which Lars von Trier created together with Thomas Vinterberg and published in the name of the 'collective of film directors' in May 1995, and has since grown into the largest production company in Denmark.

While Dogme 95 was not von Trier's first manifesto, it was the most successful one. The title of his first manifesto was *Manifesto I*, which was created in 1984 in the context of the film *The Element of Crime*, the first part of the trilogy 'Europe'. This short manifesto can be considered programmatic for his entire creation of films.

In this manifesto, the 28-year-old thereby vehemently distances himself from 'The Great Inertia' which has overcome contemporary film makers, as he argues in an allusion to the dogma of the seven deadly sins. He compares their relationship to film with a marriage turned routine, and for his generation he demands the rediscovery, or rather the reawakening of the passion for film, the 'thing' which has imparted a specific vitality to the relationship of the 'old masters of sexuality' with their films: *'fascination'* (1984: 167). Von Trier associates this desire with the request to return to early cinema. The early cinema (which Deleuze refers to as classical) for von Trier on the other hand is no longer one that is historically outdated, but owing to its vicinity to the origin, appears as young, fresh, vivid, passionate and filled with fascination, eroticism and sexuality. Hence, according to von Trier, early cinema stands for the times when the love between filmmaker and film was young, when the pleasure of creation was visible in every single image. 'We want to see', as he substantiates his request, 'religion on the screen [...] We want to see heterosexual films, made for, about and by men. We want visibility' (1984: 168).

These claims could easily be considered a young director's excessive provocations, which should not be overrated. What speaks against this interpretation, though, is the fact that von Trier was very well acquainted with early cinema, to which he intended to return. It is well known that as a film student von Trier would watch the films of the old masters over and over again. He is said to have watched Dreyer's films so often that he knew every scene by heart (see Forst 1998: 17). The repeated watching of the old masters' films for von Trier was a study of optimal tracking shots, cuts, montages, continuity and lighting.

'Ninety-nine percent of what we do', as von Trier summarised this point twenty years on in a comment on *Manderlay*, the second part of his 'USA: Land of Opportunities' trilogy, 'is reproduction. Just in a slightly different way' (2006).

What von Trier was looking for in the films of the old masters is what Deleuze calls the sensory-motor bond, the immediate effect of the movement-image on the perception which thought cannot escape. Von Trier associates this immediacy – the overpowering through movement-image – with sexuality, life and religion (faith). He establishes a relationship between the experience of being overwhelmed by the power of the movement-image, cinematographic illusion and being overcome by sexual desire, and he interprets both as immediate expressions – or 'wonderful explosions' – of life.

What stands out in comparison to Deleuze's philosophy of cinema is that thought appears neither in Trier's manifestos nor in his films as a topic or question. The first meaning of the spiritual automaton, which questions thought in its 'fantastic effort of an autonomy' (Deleuze 2005b: 252) and which challenges thought to the question of how it thinks itself, neither appears in von Trier's writings about cinema nor in his films. What Deleuze calls the 'psychological automaton', instead, plays an all the more important role: all three films of the 'Europe' trilogy, for instance, deal with the staging of dream worlds, suggestion, manipulation and hallucination, with the confrontation with the unconscious, fears of hypnosis and of the experience of not being master in one's own house. Von Trier puts this experience into practice with high technical precision. As if the actual challenge of filmmaking consisted in the perfectly staged and controlled implementation of filmic manipulation of the viewer's perception.

6. Women who sacrifice themselves

For von Trier, as we have seen, one of the most important masters of cinema is Carl Theodor Dreyer. He named Dreyer's late films *Ordet* and *Gertrud* as role models for the first part of his 'Golden Heart' trilogy, *Breaking the Waves*, which appeared in 1996 and constituted his international breakthrough.

What fascinates von Trier in Dreyer's films is the portrayal of female characters. According to von Trier, they are 'women who sacrifice themselves and thereby become stronger',[8] they resemble female Christ-like figures. Bess's self-sacrifice in *Breaking the Waves* has been portrayed by von Trier in such detail that after her exclusion from the community some boys throw stones at her, modelled on Christ's self-sacrifice. What of course distinguishes Bess's from both *Gertrud's* story and Christ's self-sacrifice is that *Breaking the Waves* at the same time depicts a melodrama which, as von Trier once summarised, 'deals with a mentally ill woman who tries to gratify the perverted desires of her voyeuristic, quadriplegic husband' (in Forst 1998: 191). In this version, Bess's story no longer recalls Dreyer's films, such as the intransigent, independent, intellectual Gertrud, or Inger who pulls all the strings of the story, but it reminds us of de Sade's Justine, Juliette's good, masochistic sister, whom Adorno and Horkheimer appropriately referred to as a 'martyr to the moral law'

(2002: 74) and who von Trier mentioned as a further source of inspiration for his creation.

7. Violence and sexuality

When *Dogville* was releasead in 2003, it was mainly the new filmic aesthetic which was discussed. The film, which was shot in a container with exclusively artificial light over a period of six weeks, with eighteen actors and no test takes, seemed to lean on Brecht's epic theatre and its didactic plays. Indeed, the story of Grace, who no one knows is the daughter of a powerful gangster boss, who will come and assist her in the annihilation of the whole town, reminds us a little of Brecht's Pirate Jenny.

The German film theorist Gertrud Koch has pointed out the fact that von Trier has 'in no way simply taken inspiration from the theatrical model, but he has cinematographically rewritten it' (2005). Thereby, as she further notes, the 'big generic topics of cinema, violence and sexuality have the same structuring function as the formal techniques, in which these motifs turn into attractive showpieces' (ibid.). This particularly applies to the close-ups of Nicole Kidman, which at times remind Koch of the close-ups of silent film star Lilian Gish. I would go even further than that and argue that *Dogville*'s filmic aesthetics look to the affection-image and the aesthetic form of Dreyer's *La passion de Jeanne d'Arc*, which was shot in 1927. This claim would, at times, seem to conflict with the use of the Steadicam and swish pan, the visual effects and the top views through which the scenery at times recalls a doll house or a computer game. In contrast to Brechtian theatre, though, the film does not derive its suggestive power from the gestures, but from the intimacy with and the vicinity to the characters which can only find an adequate expression in the filmic medium, and from the affects which von Trier captures in the close-ups of the faces on which the camera rests. From this perspective, the sparing use of props does not lean on the aesthetics of drama, but rather on the focus on what Dreyer termed the 'way of abstraction', which in turn he linked to the rejection of naturalism, which is favoured by the film's reproductive faculties. Indeed, the artificiality of the small number of props, the paths, houses and walls merely indicated by lines, and the church tower only implied by its spire, heightens the focus on the expression and fragility portrayed by Kidman in the figure of Grace. Similarly to *La passion de Jeanne d'Arc*, the space in *Dogville* is shaped through the interplay of artificial light and the movement of the camera, which captures the bodies and the expression on the faces.

In contrast to Dreyer, though, von Trier does not depict the spiritual dimension which defines the inner life of the characters; his films rather constitute an aesthetically accomplished denial of any spiritual content, which is precisely why they are particularly disturbing. Grace, for instance, who flees her father and his criminal world into the small town of Dogville in order to find a better world and to assist Tom (Paul Bettany) in the moral improvement of the town's inhabitants, simply is no Jeanne d'Arc who refuses to exchange a pair of trousers for a dress. Rather, for the sake of the observance of her moral law she deliberately accepts the role of sex slave and in this aspect resembles de Sade's Justine even more than Bess. Unlike Dreyer's films such as *Ordet* or *Gertrud*, *Dogville* is neither concerned with keeping the belief in the world in the balance, as Deleuze demanded of modern cinema, nor with discovering the 'identity of thought with choice as determination of the indeterminable' (2005b: 171), as it is not about choice. The story rather moves with relentless necessity towards the worst: first Grace's maltreatment and her regular sexual abuse, and then the annihilation of the entire town. Hence, in this respect, von Trier treats the moral problem 'theorematically' rather than 'problematically' (2005b: 169). He departs from one theory and develops it along certain axioms. Perhaps one could even go as far as claiming that *Dogville*, as Pasolini phrased it for *Salò, or the 120 Days of Sodom*, constitutes a theorem of death.

There is a scene in *Dogville* in which Grace falls into a death-like sleep. It is clearly a citation of the previously described scene from *Ordet*. We see a sleeping Grace from a bird's-eye view from above, through the contours of the canvas cover on the loading space of Bill's (Jeremy Davies) van amongst boxes with apples, lying there as in a coffin. When she wakes up she cannot remember how long she has slept, as the narrating voice says. What happened? Grace wanted to flee and had therefore given Bill a considerable sum of money. Rather than freeing her, though, after a while on the road he climbed onto the loading space and raped Grace under the light of the headlights fitted to the artificial ceiling of the container, and right underneath the artificial eye of the camera. The scene is introduced and accompanied by the first bars of Giovanni Battista Pergolesi's *Stabat Mater*, the musical version of a poem dating back to the thirteenth century which tells the story of the Passion from the Virgin Mary's point of view. The scene evokes the images of Eva, Mother Mary, Snow White and Helen. At the same time, it is a visual citation of *Ordet's* final scene, whilst simultaneously showing how far *Dogville* diverges from that spiritual automaton which Deleuze had located in Dreyer's films. Grace's cataleptic sleep, as suggested in the film, is a healthy survival strategy. Her only desire is to see the light again and upon awakening the first thing she hears is the barking of Dogville's dog. Her dead body is no mummy of thought which can be reawakened, but a sexually abused body. Dogville's inhabitants, who gather around the van and thereby recall the people who stood around Inger's coffin when she awoke, are certainly not ready for a new life with Grace; they already carry the chain with the collar which they will put around her neck in order to prevent a further attempt to escape.

8. The miracle, mystery and authority

If not a modern film in the Deleuzian sense, is *Dogville* a postmodern film? The morale of the story's ending, in which Grace transforms from Justine to Juliette, in many aspects, recalls the story of the Grand Inquisitor which Dostoyevsky tells in his novel *The Brothers Karamazov*, and therefore it evokes the nineteenth rather than the twenty-first century. Lars von Trier's dream of America is a European dream whose Christian roots are more radically deconstructed by Dostoyevsky in the story of the Grand Inquisitor than what is achieved by the films. The father's accusation of Grace in the short talk before her showdown recalls the Grand Inquisitor's reproach to the silent Christ on his reappearance: the promise of freedom and the possibility of choice he gave people were for them an unsustainable challenge. He had brought chaos and anarchy to the world and did not love people who were weak, vicious, meaningless and rebellious.

What grips people, as the Grand Inquisitor declares in accordance with the sense of Grace's father's assertions, is miracle, mystery and authority. If one loves mankind, this is what it needs to be given.

NOTES

1   For Deleuze, the crisis of the action-image, which depended on many factors, is an indication of this broken link: 'We might mention, in no particular order, the war and its consequences, the unsteadiness of the "American Dream" in all its aspects, the new consciousness of minorities, the rise and inflation of images both in the external world and in people's minds, the influence on the cinema of the new modes of narrative with which literature had experimented, the crisis of Hollywood and its old genres' (2005a: 210).

2   See Žižek's *The Pervert's Guide to Cinema*.

3   For Deleuze's account of cinematographic history and its criticism, see Bellour (1999: 44, 53, 55).

4   Artaud cited in Deleuze 2005b: 160.

5   Deleuze is quite aware that the majority of produced films follow a different path. As he acknowledges: 'Certainly, people continue to make SAS [situation – action, which modifies the situation] and ASA [action – situation, which modifies the action]: the greatest commercial successes always take that route, but the soul of the cinema no longer does' (2005a: 206).

6   'But he [Artaud]', as Deleuze writes, 'believes in the cinema as long as he considers that cinema is essentially suited to reveal this powerlessness to think at the heart of thought' (2005b: 161).

7   Deleuze addresses the changed relationship to the brain, the influence of neurophysiology and psychology in some detail in the last chapter of *Time-Image*. See p. 216 ff.

8   Lars von Trier, from an interview in the programme *Das Laboratorium des Lars von Trier* (2005).

WORKS CITED

Bellour, R. (1999) 'Denken, Erzählen. Das Kino von Gilles Deleuze', in O. Fahle and L. Engels (eds) *Der Film bei Deleuze/Le cinéma selon Deleuze*. Weimar and Paris: Verlag der Bauhaus-Universität Weimar/ Presses de la Sorbonne Nouvelles, 41–60.

Deleuze, G. (2005a [1983]) *Cinema 1. The Movement-Image*. Trans. H. Tomlinson and B. Habberjam. London: Continuum.

_____ (2005b [1985]) *Cinema 2. The Time-Image*. Trans. H. Tomlinson and R. Galeta. London: Continuum.

Deleuze G. and F. Guattari, F. (1994 [1991]) *What is Philosophy?* Trans. H. Tomlinson and G. Burchell. New York: Columbia University Press.

Forst, A. (1998) *Breaking the Dreams. Das Kino des Lars von Trier*. Marburg: Schüren.

Horkheimer M. and T. W. Adorno (2002 [1947]) *Dialectic of Enlightenment: Philosophical Fragments*. Trans. E. Jephcott. Stanford: Stanford University Press.

Koch, G. (2005) 'Auf dem Spielfeld der glücklichen Sklaven', in *Taz*, 10/11/2005, http://www.taz.de/1/archiv/archiv/?dig=2005/11/10/a0187 (accessed 15 May 2012).

Martig, C. (2008) *Kino der Irritation. Lars von Triers theologische und ästhetische Herausforderung*. Marburg: Schüren Verlag.

von Trier, L. (1984) 'Manifesto I', in C. Bainbridge, C. (2007) *The Cinema of Lars von Trier: Authenticity and Artifice*. London: Wallflower Press, 167–9.

_____ (2005) 'Interview' in *Das Laboratorium des Lars von Trier*, in *Lars von Trier's Europa Trilogy* (DVD).

_____ (2006) 'The Road to Manderlay' in L. von Trier, *Manderlay* (DVD).

Žižek, S. (2006) *The Pervert's Guide to Cinema. Parts 1–3* (DVD).

'Your Eyes Shall Be Opened and Ye Shall Be as Gods': The Director as Serpent in *Dogville*

CARMEN DELL'AVERSANO

1. What's in a name? *Dogville* as theological allegory

After Grace has been granted a two-week trial period in which to prove herself in Dogville, Tom takes her 'on a stroll down Elm street to introduce her to the town he "love[s]"' and gives her a scathing and cynical description of the inhabitants, of their faults, pettiness and hypocrisy, and which concludes with a despising look at the 'awful figurines' in the window of Ma Ginger's store, which 'say more about the people in this town than many words'. Grace retorts: 'If this is the town that you love, then you really have a strange way of showing it. All I see is a beautiful little town in the midst of magnificent mountains. A place where people have hopes and dreams even under the hardest conditions. And seven figurines that are not awful at all.' Many months later, after the people of Dogville have responded to her loving kindness with the most extreme abuse and have turned her in to her pursuers, fully expecting them to kill her, her opinion of the inhabitants of the small town is not changed: 'The people who live here are doing their best under very hard circumstances.'

Any recourse to realistic psychological categories to explain this attitude is doomed to failure: in order for what she is saying to be psychologically plausible, Grace would have to be either masochistic or feeble-minded. What I would like to argue is that any attempt to explain the character of Grace *as* a character is beside the point: Grace embodies a non-personal entity, and *Dogville*, despite all details of local colour and historical flavour, relates the workings of this entity in a completely abstract and general situation.[1] Everything Grace does, and everything that happens to her, however far-fetched, gratuitous and strained it may appear if considered from the perspective of realistic psychological narrative, makes perfect sense on a different plane: that of an allegory of the theological category of Grace and of an analysis of its workings on fallen humanity.[2]

We first get a glimpse of Grace, on the run from the shots that have just been fired at her, stealing a bone from Dogville's only dog. Tom's attention is drawn to her by its barking: 'That wasn't unusual in itself but it was the way he barked that was new. His barking was not loud, but more of a snarl, as if the danger was quite close at hand and not merely a passing raccoon or fox. As if the dog were standing face to face with a force to be taken seriously.' The Narrator's description acquires a much greater depth of meaning if we remember that the dog's name is Moses, and that 'the law was given by Moses, but grace and truth came by Jesus Christ' (*John* 1:17); it is in this sense that for Moses Grace is 'a force to be taken seriously': the 'bone of contention' between the fugitive and the dog is humanity, and Grace's increasingly puzzling attitude towards the inhabitants of the town is nothing but a continuous, stubborn affirmation, in the face of mounting evidence to the contrary, that 'sin shall not have dominion over you, for you are not under the law, but under grace' (*Romans* 6:14).

Throughout the movie, the protagonist's behaviour is a coherent, almost didactic illustration of the various facets and aspects of the theological definition of grace.[3] At the most basic level 'grace', on a subjective level, means good will, benevolence; consequently, it designates every act which proceeds from this benevolence and thus every gratuitous gift. The gratuitous nature of Grace's gifts to the town is evident from the outset:

Tom: Perhaps there's something you don't need done?
Gloria: Anything we don't need done?
Tom: Something … something that you would like done but that you don't think is necessary
Gloria: What on earth would that be?

Even though tangible material benefits may accrue through grace, these are not ends in themselves, but merely signs of grace itself. That whatever tangible services Grace provides to the town, they should only be seen as *signs* of something intangible but far more vital is – or should be – clear both from the initial stipulation ('something you don't need done') and from Grace's interpretation of the gifts she finds in her bundle when she prepares to leave town after her trial period:

Narrator: Grace pulled her bundle out from under the bureau to change into her own clothes only to discover that somebody had been in it and left a loaf of bread. Next to it was a folded sheet of paper. It was a map Tom had drawn: he had known where the bundle was and had put it there. It showed the path across the mountain, and all the dangerous spots were furnished with witty horrific little sketches. But there was more. Several people had had the same idea. They had eased gifts into the bundle for her. […] Grace had friends in Dogville. That was for sure.

To Grace, the objects she finds in her luggage are meaningful far beyond their useful materiality: they are signs of a spiritual disposition with which some of the people in Dogville have responded to the spiritual dimension of her giving.

One important aspect of the definition of a gift is that it cannot be imposed on the recipient. Accordingly, throughout the movie Grace is invariably reluctant to push herself on the people of Dogville, both as individuals ('He [Chuck] doesn't like me. And he has every right to feel that way'; 'I'll happily mind Achilles if Vera will let me. But if he doesn't like me he doesn't like me') and as a group ('I'm willing to do whatever it takes. If I have to work harder, longer hours for less pay, then I'm willing to do that, of course I am. I just wanna be sure that they wouldn't prefer that I left town'). The reverse side of this is that grace can be made unfruitful by the resistance of human free will. The most pernicious form of this resistance is the proud affirmation of human self-sufficiency, the unconditional faith in man's ability to achieve salvation by his own strength,[4] and therefore the proud refusal of any supernatural help. This is exactly the attitude the people in Dogville display from the outset:

> *Tom:* Grace, How is all going?
> *Grace:* Not very well I'm afraid.
> *Tom:* Really?
> *Grace:* No, nobody needs any help.

> *Gloria:* Mr. McKay's sight is not so good.
> *Grace:* Yes, I went to Mr. McKay. I went to Martha and to Chuck and Vera's, and nobody seems to need any help. They all think everyone else needs something and not themselves.

When they do come to accept Grace's help, they only do so under the face-saving stipulation that she will only do for them 'something they don't need done', and they will maintain this front even as they come to exploit her more and more ruthlessly.[5]

Just as the inhabitants of Dogville present themselves as people who do not need anything from anybody, Grace from the outset presents herself as someone who has nothing to give: 'I got nothing to offer them in return'; 'there is nothing I can do'). At first sight this self-characterisation might appear to be at odds with the theological centrality of grace, but actually, it expresses another basic tenet of Christian faith:

> Let this mind be in you, which was also in Christ Jesus: who, being in the form of God, thought it not robbery to be equal with God, but made himself as nothing and took upon him the form of a servant, and was made in the likeness of men; and being found in appearance as a man, he

humbled himself, and became obedient unto death, even the death of the cross. (*Philippians* 2: 5–8)

Christ's 'making himself as nothing' is a necessary prerequisite of the Incarnation, which is in turn the means by which humanity is redeemed from its sinful state: his assumption of humanity entailed a simultaneous occultation of divinity;[6] this process of lifelong self-abasement, described in the passage just quoted, is called *kenosis* (self-emptying).[7] Just like Christ's, Grace's torments are the consequence of her humility and obedience: by transposing them to another time and situation, and by making the Christ figure a woman, *Dogville* succeeds in undoing the stereotyping work of two thousand years of ritual and sacred art, and in making the horrific and sadistic component of the Passion once again perceptually salient.[8] Because Grace's torments take on a new form (she is not flogged but repeatedly raped; she is not made to carry a cross but worked to exhaustion; she is not nailed to a cross but chained to a heavy flywheel…) we can find them shocking and horrifying as we no longer can when confronted with Christ's.

But Christ's self-abasement was not an end to itself. In Christian theology *kenosis* is integrally linked to *theosis*: Christ made himself as nothing that man might become God (*2 Peter* 1:4). And the most perceptible consequence of Grace's presence in Dogville is an effect of assimilation:

You have made Dogville a wonderful place to live in. As a matter of fact somebody tells me they ran into grumpy old Chuck down the street and he was actually smiling. Well, I've never seen your smile, Grace but I will bet you I could describe it. Because it obviously has every colour that's refracted from the shiniest prism in the world. You probably have a face to match that. […] We are proud to have you among us. And we thank you for showing us who you are. Here's to you, Grace. Stay with us as long as you damn please.

In McKay's Fourth of July speech, old Chuck's smile is at the same time an imitation and a consequence of Grace's.

The link between self-abasement and redemption is nowhere more apparent than in Grace's relationship with the seven figurines which are bought with the meager earnings of her humble manual work, just as humanity is redeemed ('bought back') by Christ's Incarnation and Passion.[9] The very hideousness of the figurines, ruthlessly emphasised by Tom, and vehemently denied by Grace is a sign both of the need for grace and of its workings: grace does not find merits, but causes them; if something is given on the strength of merit it is not given by grace. The figurines are far from pretty in themselves, just as fallen man is not deserving of redemption; what makes them pretty is the action of grace:

> *Narrator:* Calling Dogville beautiful was original at least. Grace was just casting one more look at the figurines she herself would have dismissed as tasteless a few days earlier when she suddenly sensed what would best have been described as a tiny change of light over Dogville.

The symbolism could not be more transparent: as Grace begins to love Dogville, as grace begins to work on Dogville, the light changes.

Grace's whole stay in Dogville is bracketed by two changes of light:

> *Narrator:* How could she ever hate them for what was at bottom merely their weakness? She would probably have done things like those that had befallen her if she'd lived in one of these houses, to measure them by her own yardstick as her father put it. Would she not, in all honesty, have done the same as Chuck and Vera and Ben and Mrs Henson and Tom and all these people in their houses? Grace paused. And while she did, the clouds scattered and let the moonlight through; and Dogville underwent another of those little changes of light. It was as if the light, previously so merciful and faint, finally refused to cover up for the town any longer. Suddenly you could no longer imagine a berry that would appear one day on a gooseberry bush but only see the thorn that was there right now. The light now penetrated every unevenness and flaw in the buildings … and in … the people! And all of a sudden she knew the answer to her question all too well. If she had acted like them she could not have defended a single one of her actions and could not have condemned them harshly enough. It was as if her sorrow and pain finally assumed their rightful

place. No. What they had done was not good enough. And if one had the power to put it to rights, it was one's duty to do so for the sake of the other towns. For the sake of humanity. And not least for the sake of the human being that was Grace herself. [...]

Grace: Shoot them and burn down the town.

Just like the masochistic meekness she displays throughout her Calvary, Grace's abrupt change of mind in this scene cannot and should not be accounted for in psychological terms: her transformation from all-suffering victim to judge passing a death sentence, however strained and unbelievable from a psychological viewpoint, is theologically necessary and self-evident. It is no more unbelievable than the fact that Christ, after having died on the cross for all men, will come back to judge them and condemn some of them to everlasting torment:

> I believe [...] in one Lord Jesus Christ, the Son of God, the only-begotten, begotten of the Father before all ages [...]. Who for us men and for our salvation came down from heaven [...] and became man; and was crucified also for us under Pontius Pilate, and suffered [...] and sitteth at the right hand of the Father. And He shall come again with glory to judge the living and the dead; and of His kingdom there shall be no end.

2. Expanding the allegory: from the sound stage to the movie theatre

Is *Dogville*, then, nothing but a literal, however theologically sophisticated, specimen of Christian exegesis, just one more film version, however puzzlingly defamiliarised, of the Gospels, a kind of hip postmodern equivalent to Zeffirelli's kitsch masterpiece *Jesus of Nazareth*? To think so would be to neglect one fundamental aspect of the working of the artistic text: its effect on the recipient, and the position it carves out for her, and which it forces her to take up.[10]

The whole narrative of the film is acted out on a single sound stage, where the houses and streets of the small mountain town are marked by lines and names chalked on the floor and day and night are symbolised by the alternation between a white and a black side-scene. The set is minimal: the walls and doors of the buildings are absent (even though their closing is marked by sound effects), and the props are sparse. Because of this, the camera moves unhindered through the whole narrative world, entering and exiting public and private spaces, passing through streets and homes.

The most immediate association of a reasonably literate audience faced with this quasi-theatrical, decidedly anti-realistic set design would probably be to a Brechtian estrangement from the conventions of narrative cinema, to a pointedly self-reflexive presentation highlighting the constructed status of the narrative. This is self-evidently true, but only part of the story. A more pertinent reading of the set design must take into account the way in which the audience first comes in touch with it, through an opening shot filmed from above which comes down from a height to encompass the whole world of the film, from the street leading into the town to the abandoned mine and the steep path leading up the mountain, to the town proper, with all its streets and houses, and with all its inhabitants, offering us a panoptical view of the story about to unfold. This completely vertical view, which must have been fairly challenging to accomplish technically, is accompanied by the first words of the Narrator, who is not only omniscient but serenely detached and ironically objective. Both the Narrator's voice − a calm, knowing presence − and the visual perspective which makes everything visible at all times will accompany us throughout the movie, framing our perception of the narrative and of the world where it takes place: the first time Grace is raped she is inside Chuck's house; the second time she is lying hidden under a tarp on Ben's truck; both times we get to see past wall and covering, and achieve direct access to what is really happening.

Together, narrative voiceover and visual perspective frame a God-like point of view with which, from the opening scene onwards, we are called upon to identify perceptually, while the vicissitudes of Grace, her endearing humility and unfailing kindness, the dignity with which she refrains from imposing on anyone, and the inexplicably brutal treatment she receives at the hands of the town's inhabitants, frame the position with which we are called upon to identify emotionally. Because of the way the narrative is presented, the cognitive position we as viewers assume from the outset to the last scene is one of impassible omniscience, while our emotional positioning shifts from a perception of ourselves as divinely innocent and unjustly wronged to a feeling of God-like justice which entitles us to pass definitive judgement on other human beings: as the narrative unfolds, we identify first with Grace's suffering, and thus with Christ's passion, and then with Grace's revenge, and thus with Christ as judge.[11]

It may not be immediately obvious that this reaction to the film is nothing but the most extreme and intense restatement of one of its central themes: arrogance.[12] The proper position a human viewer should take up is not that of Grace, but that of her tormentors: by virtue of being human, any viewer is heir to the same faults and blindness that the inhabitants of Dogville demonstrate throughout the movie, and in the same situation would probably have reacted in a very similar way. Grace uses circumstances to exonerate humans ('A deprived childhood and a homicide really isn't necessarily a homicide, right? The only thing you can blame is circumstances'); we use the character and nature of Dogville's inhabitants to exonerate ourselves, thinking (and maybe even believing) that we would never have acted like Chuck or Tom (or Eichmann…) in similar circumstances. The first attempt at exoneration is refuted quite explicitly, first by Grace's father ('If you say so, Grace. But is their best really good enough? Do they love you?'), and then by Grace's own definitive judgement of the town. The second one is refuted in a less direct way by the Narrator's concluding words about the first meeting in the mission house:

Narrator: No more words were spoken at the town meeting in the mission house. But it had been decided they all felt that the fugitive would be given two weeks. And they would all be able to look at themselves in the mirror and know that they had done what they could indeed, and perhaps more than most people would have done.

Here the people of Dogville are shown employing the most basic cognitive trick of self-exculpation, which consists in measuring oneself always against 'most people' (conveniently imagined so as to embody more or less serious ethical faults) and never against an absolute ethical standard. While watching the film, by assuming the behaviour of the inhabitants of Dogville as the standard against which to measure herself, the viewer gets to enjoy the same unfounded feeling of moral superiority.

The point is that, from a theological perspective, both attempts at exoneration are equally self-serving and futile: human nature and the human situation are not causes in themselves, but consequences of the Fall; the real reason why fallen humanity behaves as it does is that it is fallen, and by refusing grace it chooses to stay that way. But a major determinant of the human refusal of grace is the particular form of pride which allows us to believe that, as Grace says after her fruitless attempts to offer her help to the people of Dogville, 'everyone else needs something and not [our]selves'. However, in the viewer this particularly insidious and pernicious form of pride is the consequence of the positions (both cognitive and emotional) into which she has been pushed by the structural and technical choices made by the director. The fact that we, as viewers, simply by virtue of watching the movie as it has been conceived and filmed, become entangled in a position of proud self-righteousness which makes it impossible to recognise our own need for grace, and thus to accept and experience salvation, is the artistic equivalent of another, much older, rhetorical manipulation:

> Now the serpent was more subtle than any beast of the field which the lord God had made. And he said unto the woman: Yea, hath not God said, ye shall not eat of every tree of the garden? And the woman said unto the serpent: we may eat of the fruit of the trees of the garden. But of the fruit of the tree which is in the midst of the garden, God hath said, Ye shall not eat it, neither shall ye touch it, lest ye die. And the serpent said unto the woman: Ye shall not surely die. For God doth know that in the day ye eat thereof, then your eyes shall be opened, and ye shall be as gods, knowing good and evil. (*Genesis* 3: 1–5)

In our experience as viewers our eyes are indeed opened: the set design and camera's point of view allows us to witness every detail of Grace's treatment at the hands of the townspeople; the narrative voiceover makes us familiar with their hidden weaknesses and petty thoughts. And our identification with Grace, both as a victim and as a judge, makes us 'as gods'. But this superficial realisation of the serpent's promise comes at the expense of its most profound meaning: far from 'knowing good and evil', we fraudulently identify with the goodness of Grace and become blind to the evil in ourselves. By watching *Dogville* we do not experience spiritual progress or elevation but, on the contrary, succumb to a temptation; to a temptation which is the oldest temptation of all because it is the only temptation there is: that of believing that by our own merits we can transcend our humanity, that by our own wits we can escape our creaturely nature and identify with God. However striking and detailed the parallels between Grace and grace, and between her story and the key moments of the New Testament – the Incarnation, Passion and Last Judgement, *Dogville* is ultimately about the ever-presentness, and the inevitability, of the Fall, which it reenacts not on-screen, but in the movie house, with the audience as Adam and Eve – and with Lars von Trier as the Serpent.

NOTES

1   Tom rejects Grace's suggestion to name the town in the story he has just started saying 'Wouldn't work. No, it wouldn't work. It's got to be universal. Lot of writers make that mistake you see.' Since everywhere in the movie Grace is right and Tom is wrong, this is a quite transparent hint at the universal nature of the town, and at the universal thrust of the story.

2   Lars von Trier explicitly acknowledges a general connection between film and religion in an interview with Ole Michelsen: 'All the classic forms of religion contain the basic elements that I would like to see within films as well' (in Michelsen 2003: 12). More specifically, he converted to Catholicism in 1989 (Lumholdt 2003: XXII; it is not clear when von Trier's exactly converted to Catholicism, as the different dates provided in his interviews also demonstrate); it is reasonable to presume that on that occasion he underwent some kind of religious instruction, and thus became familiar with at least the main tenets of Catholic dogma, among them the role and effects of grace. Some knowledge of details would, of course,

be extremely useful. I cannot help but be intensely puzzled by the complete lack of interest which has been uniformly shown by critics and interviewers for this aspect of his biography which, judging from the chronology of his works, would appear to have exerted a far from negligible influence on his poetics: the so-called 'Golden Heart' trilogy, whose first movie, *Breaking the Waves* came out in 1996, marks a definite departure from his previous manner, both in style and technique and in content, and depicts women as Christ figures in various forms of the Passion; both *Dogville* and *Manderlay* are theological allegories; but the most telling piece of evidence for the primacy of Christianity in von Trier's poetics, and for the Christ identity of his female protagonists, is its latest, disphoric avatar, *Antichrist*, where the woman-as-Christ theme is reversed, but not forsaken.

3   The following information about the concept of grace comes from *The Catholic Encyclopedia*, 1909.

4   Even though the technical theological term for this attitude is Pelagianism, its cultural roots are in the ancient Stoic ideal of virtue, *autarcheia*, which proudly attributed to the wise man the ability to achieve perfection unaided. It is therefore probably not by coincidence that Stoicism appears in one of the most emotionally and theoretically fraught scenes in the movie:

> *Grace:* Vera, remember how I taught your children…
> *Vera:* What?
> *Grace:* Remember how happy you were when I…
> *Vera:* When you what?
> *Grace:* When I taught your children about the doctrine of stoicism and they finally understood it.
> *Vera:* All right, for that I'm gonna be lenient I'm going to break two of your figurines first. And if you can demonstrate your knowledge of the doc-trine of stoicism by holding back your tears I'll stop. Have you got that?

5   One particularly telling detail is that in the end the townspeople resort to Tom to rid them of Grace; since she is only in town because she has been brought back when she tried to run away, and has been made to wear an 'escape prevention mechanism', on the face of it nothing would be easier than getting rid of her by simply letting her go. The real problem for the inhabitants of Dogville is not simply how to get rid of Grace, but how to get rid of her without giving up the

considerable material benefits which accrue from her presence, which they do not feel they can mention, even to themselves, because they 'don't need them'. Tom's solution (stated obliquely and hypocritically as is customary for him: 'None of us feel able to accept money for just helping people; I mean, not unless it would make you feel better to divest yourself') is to surrender Grace to her pursuers, in order to reap the 'reward' he has been promised, which will serve as a compensation for the unavailability of her material services from then on.

6   Unlike Christ, Grace is not sent by her father, but runs away from him, and is first seen in Dogville after 'the sound of gunfire directed against her person'. This might be seen as adumbrating an uncannily Gnostic version of the Incarnation, where Christ's humanity is a consequence of the death of His divinity. This interpretation would seem to be confirmed by her father's words to Tom: 'I'm looking for a girl. She may have made her way to your town in her confusion. I don't want any harm to come to her. You see, she's very precious to me.'

7   The source for the information about kenosis is *The Catholic Encyclopedia*, 1909. Self-emptying is also the dominant motive in von Trier's favourite childhood book: *Guld Hjerte* (*Golden Heart*) tells the story of a little girl who goes into the woods fully clothed and with full pockets; as she proceeds, she gives up all her belongings and all her clothes; yet, whenever someone draws her attention to her spoliation, she invariably replies 'I'll be fine anyway', and continues to do so even after she is left completely naked and destitute. In an interview with Stig Bjorkman (1996), von Trier cites this tale as the formative story of his life.

8   I cannot help being reminded of the only good joke in Bob Fosse's *Lenny*, about how, if Christ's martyrdom had taken place in our century, pupils in Catholic schools would be running around with tiny electric chairs dangling from their necks.

9   *Narrator:* And now [...] she received wages; not much, but enough to save up for the first of the tiny china figurines from the row of seven that had stood for so long gathering dust in the window of the store. And she dreamed that in time she would be able to acquire them all.

10 That the meaning of the artistic text is to be identified with its effect is the theoretical starting point of reader-response criticism; see Iser (1976); that any form of interaction defines for each of the participants positions to be taken up is the foundation of positioning theory; see Harré and van Langenhove (1999).

11 Here (as throughout the chapter) I am considering the positions made available

by the text for the 'implied reader' to take up, and not the responses of individual audiences or audience members: we as individuals may not be able to, or refuse to, identify with Grace, but this does not change the fact that the structure of the text asks us to.

12 The first thing Grace says about herself is 'I was raised to be arrogant'; she reacts to Tom's 'Trojan horse' to captivate Chuck with 'You sound so arrogant! Arrogance is the worst thing!', and in the end we learn that her fight with her father, which had precipitated her arrival in Dogville, had been provoked by her calling him 'arrogant', and that one main reason why he has been looking for her is to tell her 'But that is exactly what I don't like about you. It is you that is arrogant!'

WORKS CITED

Bjorkman, S. (1996) 'Naked Miracles,' *Sight and Sound*, 6, 10 (October), 10–16.

The Catholic Encyclopedia. Vol. 6. New York: Robert Appleton Company, 1909. At: http://www.newadvent.org/cathen/06689a.htm (accessed 27 November 2009).

Harré, R. and L. von Langenhove (eds) (1999) *Positioning Theory: Moral Contexts of Intentional Action*. Oxford: Blackwell.

Iser, W. (1976) *Der Akt des Lesens*. München: Wilhelm Fink Verlag.

Lumholdt, J. (ed.) (2003) *Lars von Trier: Interviews*. Jackson: University Press of Mississippi.

Michelsen, O. (2003) 'Passion is the Lifeblood of Cinema', in J. Lumholdt (ed.) (2003) *Lars von Trier: Interviews*. Jackson: University Press of Mississippi, 5–12.

Integrity and Grace

MAXIMILIAN DE GAYNESFORD

> We must consider not only the degree of unification of all the elements
> into a 'unity of sentiment', but the quality and kind of the emotions to be
> unified, and the elaborateness of the pattern of unification.
> — T. S. Eliot (1933: 37)

The inquiry which *Dogville* has it at heart to provoke in an audience responsive to its narrative lines and sensitive to the temperaments and dispositions of its characters and their moral development through circumstance and interaction, seems not only to arise from, but to be identical with the problem it has it in mind to pose for itself, as an act of creative filmmaking which attempts to expose and exploit the nature of film as such and, where possible, to extend its capacity for imaginative disclosure: namely, how it is possible for an individual, be it a human person (like Grace) or an artistic work (like *Dogville*), to attain and preserve that wholeness and unity necessary to count as the individual it is, true to itself and its condition, single and entire, integrated, authentic and complete, in the face of those pressures to separate, fragment or play false to itself which arise from internal tensions and external temptations, from the mutual impacts and influences of events, states of affairs and relations, from the particular situations in which that individual floats or is fixed, from the multiplicity of obstacles which the combinations of these forces construct, and from the opportunities which these combinations afford? In short, *Dogville* raises the question of how integrity is possible. And if Stanley Cavell is right, that film criticism ought always to be 'forced back upon a faithfulness to nothing but our experience and a wish to communicate it' (1979: 20), then it is primarily on this issue that criticism of *Dogville* should focus.

1. Integrity questions

It helps to begin with illustrations. Consider two parallel scenes, each emblematic in their own right, but more sharply revealed in the light of the other. In the first, a woman stands apart, a figure of great weakness and frailty. A deal is being struck behind her back with which she will have no choice but to comply. She is to be a slave in all but name, to live at the call of another, to carry out menial tasks for them, to service their sexual desires, and all with only the smallest provision for her own needs. What little food, housing and free time she has will be dependent on the good will of those she serves. The one who delivers her into this bondage is the one responsible for her welfare and under whose protection she lives. Her enslavement is presented as a hard-won deal, for her own benefit, and for which she should be grateful. She humbly consents, giving her life for another, in the pathos of fully knowing and feeling fully that she is giving it up for too little. In the second scene, the woman standing apart is a figure of intense inner authority and outward power. She has struck a deal with a gang of murderers and cutthroats and they are carrying out her orders, systematically destroying the community which has housed her and given her a role, but which has also betrayed, abused and humiliated her. The members of this community are put to death, one by one, until the last to remain living is the man most responsible for her previous state. After a short verbal interchange, she picks up a weapon and executes him herself.

The first description is true not only to *Dogville* but to the opening scene of Federico Fellini's *La Strada*. In that film, the woman (Gelsomina) is subsequently forced to leave her mother's protection and to live out her servitude on the road, in the motorcycle-caravan of a circus strongman (Zampanò). In *Dogville*, the woman (Grace) is forced to live out her servitude in the place it was arranged, with the man (Tom) who claims to love her and those to whom he has enslaved her. And the second description is true not only to *Dogville* but to the final scene of Fritz Lang's *Die Niebelungen: Kriemhild's Rache*. In both, the execution is simple and disturbingly elegant. In the latter, the woman (Kriemhild) then falls lifeless to the ground, having accomplished the task with which she has identified herself. In *Dogville*, the woman (Grace) gets into a car with the other gangsters and drives away.

This is one way of introducing the central problem raised by the narrative of *Dogville*. The final 'chapter' (Nine) effects a radical break with what has gone before, a rupture that has its elements of rapture, the eschatological event which puts an end to a period of terrible tribulation with the return of an authoritative figure and the restoration of order, bringing a world to its completion and fulfilment.[1] And the questions arising are issues of integrity. Two in particular are worth noting. First, is it possible to regard the narrative as consistent and coherent in a way that constructs or sustains its integrity as an artistic work when it begins and develops as kin in form and thematic content to a film like *La Strada* and ends as a variation on the holocaust of *Kriemhild's Rache*? The integrity question here is whether the story which *Dogville* tells undergoes so radical a change that its beginnings do not belong to its ending, and its ending is divorced from its beginnings. Second, is it possible to regard Grace as the representation of a person, the same character over time, in a way that achieves or maintains her integrity as a united and whole human individual? The integrity question here is whether Grace undergoes so brutal and abrupt a change in nature and temperament that she loses the wholeness and unity necessary to be the individual she is, true to herself and her condition.

Of course, if we are 'forced back upon a faithfulness to nothing but our experience', it may be that our encounter with *Dogville* convinces us of the integrity of both narrative and character, their plausibility as unified and united individuals. But that does not solve the question of integrity; it simply makes it more precise. Given the deep rupture, how is that conviction to be justified? Alternatively, our experience of the film may cause us to doubt that either narrative or character have integrity; we may point to this rupture in the last 'chapter' as evidence. But this simply moves the questions of integrity one stage back. For the appearance of an integrated film and a unified character may be merely that, an illusion. But how is that deception to be explained? Pointing to some clever subterfuge of plot or filmic presentation, played at the expense of the audience, is unlikely to be sufficient. For if a trick of this depth and complexity is to be brought off, it would require some connivance on the part of the viewer, whether or not they are entirely conscious and self-aware of their collaboration. And that is simply to raise the question of integrity again. How is that connivance to be justified? *Dogville*, of course, has already made that issue salient. For if the audience possesses a willingness to be manipulated, to place its trust in what it knows or suspects is not to be trusted, then it takes up a similar position in moral space to that staked out by, and for, the citizens of *Dogville*.

2. Salience and cinematography

Dogville also issues a more deeply self-reflective invitation to inquire into the nature of integrity. The stripped-down static interior stage-set and theatre-like lighting and sound worlds impose conditions on what can be seen and heard for which viewers have not been prepared by their prior experience of the relevant and inter-related art-forms of cinema and theatre, and with which they are evidently not meant to become comfortable in the course of experiencing this film; the effects are simply too pervasive, too consistent, too *persistent* to be ignored. These self-imposed conditions of the *mise-en-scène* – the set, its props, the lighting, the positioning of the actors, their possibilities of movement, and so on – operate as systematic restrictions, 'obstructions', which the film forces itself to negotiate. They are immediately obvious to the audience as obstructions and are made to remain salient as such throughout.

Many of the sounds, for example, are obviously produced apart from the images, and in such a way that they must be experienced as *simulated* sounds. The noise of doors closing or being knocked could not be produced by doors where there are no doors. Much of the lighting is similarly made to be experienced as *artificial* illumination. The sun rises and sets with the flicking of switches, as do changes of mood; character changes dawn abruptly over the township with the use of filters which change the intensity and colour of this lighting. Other features stand out stark and revealed by being left apparently half-done. So the set proclaims itself as a set because some but not all the usual illusionary devices are used. The costumes and props create full temporal and geographical alienation because they make the film feel as if it is set neither in the here-and-now nor in the there-and-then, but in some other sphere inaccessible from either of these space/time points. Given the restrictions on camera-movement, there can be little attempt to maintain the illusion that the camera is brought to the action; most of what we experience feels as if it is produced *for* the camera and not simply in front of it. These conditions function as a challenge, a provocation to the audience: *why* was it necessary to present the narrative and its central characters in this way?[2]

It is in keeping with the thematic content of the film, its concern with the gracious, to seek the reason for such conditions in the effects they produce, trusting that intention is what matches the one with the other. *Dogville* resists assimilation of the viewer's point of view to their point of focus, that surrender of the viewer's critical and self-critical faculties for the sake of narrative ease which some films set out to secure by allowing or encouraging the attention to be devoted to *what* is being shown, thus suppressing self-conscious awareness of the *way* in which it is being shown and the perspective *from which* it is being shown. The chalk lines that represent plants, buildings and animals, the off-stage sounds that accompany gestures of knocking, the dimming and flicking of switches that mark sunrise, nightfall and the changes of season, combine with the always-obvious presence of the camera and the occasional jump-cut to draw attention away from *what* is being seen and heard, via the *way* it is seen and heard, to the fact *that* it is being shown and presented, a performance that has been edited and fashioned so as to be rendered interpretable. So that, perhaps, is the answer to the riddle: it is to encourage and sustain these kinds of attention that *Dogville's mise-en-scène* mounts its strategy of obstruction.

But a strategy based on keeping taut the audience's self-conscious self-awareness of itself *as* an audience risks an equal and opposite disaster: assimilating their point of focus to their point of view. At this other extreme of the possibilities available, the audience's awareness of what is being shown is suppressed or rendered inert by the self-conscious attention they are obliged to devote to its ways of being shown. Neither pole is attractive; but it can seem that there is no way to avoid the dangers of the one without having to embrace the drawbacks of the other. The way to dismount from this perilous see-saw is to find a way of integrating the different modes of attending, keeping both what is being shown and the way it is being shown salient to the audience. This is an integrity problem of course: how to integrate point of view with point of focus.

One solution is to make salient what is shown by making salient the way it is being shown. And that, so it would appear, is precisely the method adopted by *Dogville*. If the attempt succeeds, *Dogville* issues a demonstrative corrective to Robert Bresson, who famously assumed that there must be an absolute distinction between a film that exploits the nature of film as such (his definition of 'cinematography') and a film that exploits the resources of theatre (his definition of 'cinema') (1997: 13–44). *Dogville* employs what Bresson detests: 'stars', a theatre-stage, props and other simulated items, and constant appeals to suspend disbelief (e.g. that what is obviously a drape over the camera is a tarpaulin over Grace, hiding on the truck with the apples). Bresson's reason for detesting such 'photographed theatre' is that he believed it must fail to expose and exploit the nature of film. In order to succeed where he believed 'cinema' must fail, he used devices which somewhat alienate an audience used to slickness of delivery, most particularly his 'models' (rather than actors), whose self-consciousness adds a deliberately non-realistic dimension to the experience of what is said or done, and his doubling (even trebling) of key events, so that what the audience is told (and sometimes also sees written) is regularly followed, in apparently redundant fashion, by what they are shown. What Bresson does not see, and *Dogville* reveals, is that a film can exploit the resources of theatre in so contrived a way as to achieve the very effects his models and doublings were meant to achieve: by deepening the audience's appreciation of the narrative and its development, its ability to perceive and be discriminating about the film's broadly moral and aesthetic content; by heightening its awareness of form, of the nature of film as such, of the contributory media on which film depends, and of the modes of their combination. In short, it is possible for 'cinema' to enter into the condition of 'cinematography'. And that is precisely how *Dogville* integrates point of view with point of focus.

3. Narrative and grace

So the problem of integrity not only binds the narrative and thematic content of *Dogville* to its characterisation but functions as a basic structural device in the film, one that explains and seeks to justify its aesthetic rationale. What light this proposal sheds on the poetic structure of the film can best be appreciated by pointing out details of its narrative.

The story is told in a self-consciously literary and quasi-edifying way, not unlike a Fielding novel, with an omniscient, rather sardonic narrator, chapters, and a moral design whose features are articulated at every salient point by a number of devices, in particular the commentary (spoken and musical[3]) and the chapter-titles. These various features envelop the film, giving it an appearance of unity and completeness. But the disparity between the refinement of the music and the grim events depicted alerts the audience to the possibility that this unity is specious and imposed. The spoken commentary heightens this effect, preserving a constancy of tone and manner throughout which clashes increasingly with what is being described, the narrator remaining seemingly unshocked by the degradations that the townspeople inflict on Grace and, in the final chapter, by the retributions that she exacts. His words depict what occurs in an equally jarring way, sometimes exaggerating the value of a commonplace act, sometimes dulling descriptions of actions so that virtues and vices are made to appear almost (but never quite) indistinguishable. What these commentaries say and what they are taken to mean undermine each other, the one attempting to draw together a unified conception of a unified story, while the other unravels both.

Moses announces the coming of Grace, a first toll of the eschatological bell whose last echo will be heard at the very end of the story, uniting beginning and end, when Moses alone is left alive, barking as the camera descends on him. No one comes to *Dogville* except through Moses, but Grace's appearance is prepared for by Tom's appreciation of the situation, his sense that the township needs a 'gift'. He may take himself to mean by this that the community needs something to stir it out of its complacency. But what he desires is a platform from which to address the community, and that is the gift Grace's arrival offers him. He soon seeks more, of course, and under the influence of desire and Grace's slightly patronising encouragement, is brought to agree that he loves her (Chapter Four). There is some doubt, never wholly resolved in the course of the film, as to whether he just agrees out of laziness (because he knows that what he does feel for her is altogether more complex and to be expressed in a more personalised way than this hackneyed form allows), or inadequacy (because he lacks the emotional self-awareness to know what he feels, the analytical skills to discriminate, and the courage to express himself), or self-interest (because he knows that his desire for her would be off-putting if expressed as frankly as sincerity would force him to express it). But his feelings are certainly not so simple that her requital evokes the least joy or satisfaction in him. We are not made to feel that it is sincerity that prevents him hiding this absence from Grace.

The low, discordant tones of 'revelation' grow in reverberation through the scenes that follow until they find temporary resolution in Tom's final betrayal of Grace four chapters later. He knows that she knows he lacks the sensitivity and intelligence for the books he is planning to write, and he recognises that living with this knowledge would prevent him composing them. Presumably it is honest of him that he never appeals to his love for her or hers for him; or it may simply be that, by the end, he knows there is no hope of this strategy succeeding. He tries to create a justification without directly attempting to justify himself by using an alienating effect that is as distancing as the *mise-en-scène* itself: if we think of what has happened as a story, it is at least an edifying one, a story that says so much about what it is to be human. It is immediately after this that Grace returns to the car and her father correctly interprets her remark as the order to destroy the town. Tom may reveal some ironic recognition of his own failure as a writer-to-be when he congratulates Grace on her 'illustration' ('D'you think I could *allow* myself to use it as an inspiration in my writing?'), as if it is scruples which block him, an enviable fastidiousness, and not lack of ability. But nothing in this little speech prevents

Grace killing the man she is in love with (or at least with whom she has believed herself in love). Tom's character stands out most clearly as the negation of integrity – insincere, dishonest, alienated, corrupt – and against which the character who seems most closely to approximate that quality stands out in turn.

Grace, in her poverty, offers the town little more than her name and what it signifies. But by virtue of direct and indirect allusion, the various senses of that name accumulate a burden of significance over the course of the film which may be sufficient to carry the ending with it, creating conviction in an audience made circumspect or hesitant by the ruptures of Chapter Nine. It is for her pleasing qualities, her charms, and her capacity to produce a favourable impression, that Grace is appreciated by the community, whose spokesman is McKay in his self-consciously charming, halting speech. But before she can be approved in this way, Grace has first to appear to the community in another sense of her name: as a favour, an act of kindness, and a benefit. Yet this is a lie of course. The work she does for them is treated as payment, or repayment, for their consideration: in effect, for their silence. They ask her to work at what they do not need but would nevertheless like to have done for them, recalling that sense of her name which reappears in 'grace-note': an embellishment, attractive but inessential. But this is a deliberate falsehood also: the various members of the community come very quickly to depend on her and to regard what she does as indispensable. And what she offers are necessities of a deeper sort, for example, the 'provocation' of McKay, which acts like an inflection of miracle-literature: taking a blind man and making him see again – not the world but himself; seeing himself as others see him by making him see that she sees he cannot see; enabling him to come to some kind of terms with himself by making him see that she knows he knows she knows this.

Under the ever-increasing exploitation of her time, energy, body and emotional life, Grace becomes further alienated from that which her name signifies. For grace is a free gift, offered without charge, unlimited and liberating. But Grace is increasingly bound, constrained, controlled and forced to act against her will. This inevitably occasions signs of alienation, not only from others, but from herself: an inability to identify herself with the one who acts as she must now act, who thinks as she must now think, of which the symptoms are a hesitancy about what to do or think, an ineptness about what she says and does, a constant tiredness, and a desire for oblivion. The possibility that she might use her sufferings as a means to safeguard her identity, or at least to reconstruct something from its fragmented state, is destroyed with the figurines. This is in part because they have functioned as a kind of covenant with the town, a sign that her life there, however miserable, has value and significance – indeed, that it is her suffering that is meaningful about her life there. But it is also because the figures have come to be surrogate children for her. We know this, not only because the narrator describes them as 'the offspring of the meeting between the township and her', but because when she makes the punishment fit the crime, this is the analogy that naturally and immediately occurs to her: children for figurines.

In ordering their execution, it is Grace herself who chooses to act against what her name denotes, refusing to be gracious or merciful, sympathetic or forgiving. She says 'do the kids first', where that verb is either an awful surrender to gangster effortlessness or an honest identification with and ownership of what she has organised. She says of the mother 'I owe her that', where the remark is equally ambiguous. Is it sadism that she owes: in increasing the mother's agony by making her children's deaths seem to depend partly on her weakness? Or is it a chance she owes: in that that at least some of those precious to her should be saved? Or is it a lesson in Stoicism she owes? That is how Tom interprets it; he calls the killings and destruction her 'illustration', and praises its clarity. If so, it is a harsh and self-defeating demonstration: to teach a lesson and at the same time prevent those taught learning from it; indeed, to choose an action that accomplishes both simultaneously. But perhaps this punishment has a certain justice to it also as the township, after all, has been keen that she be 'taught', but by means which alienate her from herself, and thus prevent her from learning. This series of acts constitutes Grace's refusal to be herself, the embodiment of grace. But at the last, she at last returns to her former state, one in which her name again describes her. The transformation is something like the magical lifting of a curse in a fairy tale. For it is with the archetypal *coup de grâce* that she despatches Tom, one that causes him the very pain it puts him out of.[4] By this deed, 'grace' again holds true of her, and she reacquires her right to her name.

4. Integrity and uniqueness

So if a pun holds the clue to *Dogville*, then that would solve one of our integrity problems. Far from undermining Grace's unity and wholeness as a character, it is the rupture for which she is responsible in Chapter Nine which restores her to integrity. But perhaps there is more to this than a play on words. By the end of the film, Grace is certainly exercising a capacity for self-determination which renders what she says and does consistent with her conception of herself; she is no longer alienated, either from herself or from her situation. So there is a certain unity to her, a completeness of action and reaction, which are regularly identified with integrity. Is this not a good and sufficient reason to suppose the rupture restores her to integrity? The problem is that there are three deep disagreements in our understanding of integrity, and the case of Grace exposes each of them.

Some are absolutist about integrity. It is a condition or state that can be corrupted or broken; once gone, it could not be recovered. So, for example, the first recorded use of the phrase in English (OED) is to describe the Virgin Mary, and it glosses 'integritee' as 'hir maydenhod'. Others, on the contrary, do not merely allow for such 'falls from grace', but insist on the kinds of change that may require them. They regard integrity as a completion, a fulfilment; so it cannot be something one merely preserves, but must be something one achieves in the face of obstacles and failures. Grace then functions as something of a test case. Those who would deny that she ends the film a person of integrity may do so because they are absolutists about integrity; those who take the contrary view may do so because they hold the contrary position.

The second disagreement is orthogonal to the first. Some think integrity is a purely formal quality, a condition or state of wholeness that depends on being consistent and committed. Being consistent means being consistent *about* something; being committed means being committed *to* something. But formalists deny that one's integrity depends in any way on *what* one is consistent about or committed to. Others, on the contrary, are substantialist about integrity: they insist that it is a state or condition which is dependent on content as well as form. If personal integrity requires being consistent and committed, it is also a matter of what one is consistent about and committed to. For example, it may be that there are only certain kinds of actions that the person of integrity can do, certain kinds of people they can be committed to, and certain kinds of projects they can support. There is a familiar test case, which is vivid enough (if not examined too closely). Suppose we are asked whether there could be Nazis of integrity. Those who think what matters for integrity is the nature of the principles one is committed to as well as the quality of one's commitment, will answer 'No'. Those who think the quality of one's commitment alone is what matters may be prepared to accept the possibility. Grace, of course, also functions as a test case. Her hard-won capacity for self-determination, which renders her actions fully consistent again with her beliefs and intentions, is bought at a certain price: by identification with and commitment to her father's business. If one is a formalist, this will not detract from a willingness to describe her as a person of integrity. If one is a substantialist, it will. T. S. Eliot announces his allegiance to the latter party in the epigraph: we must consider the 'quality and kind' of elements being unified, as well as the fact of their unification.

The third divergence occurs when we consider strength and weakness. Generally speaking, philosophical accounts assume that integrity is only possible for the strong: those intellectually robust enough to have formulated projects; those psychologically strong enough to commit to them; those powerful enough to put those projects into practice enough of the time for them to remain viable; those who are able to act according to their own aims rather than those of others; those who are powerful enough to keep their own 'possessions' (given a suitably wide definition of what these may be) intact; and so on. Whereas the more familiar view is that the very paradigm of the person of integrity is one who is weak and vulnerable, poor, perhaps near death or dying, but with an unshakeable resolve. The unshakeableness, without which the integrity would not come into focus, is precisely predicated on the fact that the person is not simply under threat of being beaten down, but has in all significant respects *been* beaten down. It is precisely in possessing themselves in a certain way when no longer strong or powerful that they are, and are recognised as being, persons of integrity. Grace, of course, may count as a person of integrity on both views, but not at the same time. Those who take the first view will see in her final act a figure of integrity and will regard the story as a triumph. Those who take the second view will regard the story as a tragedy. Grace loses her integrity, her self-possession, either because it is taken from her by those who exploit her and succeed in alienating her from herself, or because she herself renounces it in the very actions which restore her to complete self-determination.

By making Grace a test case in each of these three areas, *Dogville* raises the very questions about the nature and value of integrity which lie at the heart of philosophical debate on the subject. This is not the place to resolve these questions because the film itself attempts only to raise them. But it is relevant to note how uniquely *Dogville* suits itself to the task. For there are many films which take as their theme the persecution of individuals by small or enclosed communities, the admirable responses of those individuals to their situation, and the consequential raising of integrity-relevant questions. But none manage their narrative and thematic content so adroitly as to test common conceptions about integrity in as many areas of disagreement as *Dogville*.

La Strada (Fellini), *Mouchette* (Bresson), *Faustrecht der Freiheit* (*Fox and his Friends*, Rainer Werner Fassbinder), *Angst essen Seele auf* (*Fear Eats the Soul*, Fassbinder) and *Dancer in the Dark* (von Trier) all force us to ask whether integrity is possible, or indeed *only* possible, from a position of weakness. But because the central characters remain innocent and essentially victims, these films do not raise the question of whether integrity is an absolute notion and whether it is as the formalist conceives of it. *La Terra Trema* (*The Earth Will Tremble*, Visconti), *Pickpocket* (Bresson), *The Trial of Joan of Arc* (Bresson), *Mutter Küsters Fahrt zum Himmel* (*Mother Küsters Goes to Heaven*, Fassbinder; his first ending) and *Breaking the Waves* (von Trier) all force us to ask whether integrity depends on the nature of the reasons for which one acts, or simply on one's acting in a consistent and committed way. But because the central characters achieve their ends by sacrifice and surrender, these films do not raise the question of whether integrity is possible from a position of strength or whether it is as the absolutist conceives of it. *Le Corbeau* (*The Raven*, Henri-George Clouzot), *Un condamné à mort s'est échappé ou Le vent souffle où il veut* (*A Man Escaped*, Bresson), *Rocco e i suoi fratelli* (*Rocco and his Brothers*, Luchino Visconti) and *The Wrong Man* (Hitchcock) all force us to ask whether integrity is an incorruptibility that is preserved or a wholeness that is achieved. But because the central characters meet what success they have through strength, and because they achieve their ends by moral (or at least morally innocent) means, these films do not raise the question of whether integrity is as the formalist or substantialist achieves it.

In *Die verlorene Ehre der Katharina Blum* (*The Lost Honour of Katharina Blum*, Schlöndorff), the central character is innocent, persecuted, alienated from herself, and chooses to kill her tormentor, just as in *Dogville*. But the retribution she exacts is considerably more limited, and she is in turn punished for it, being imprisoned and separated from her lover. So the film smudges the issue, treating two possibilities as if they were one. For if we regard her as a person of integrity, it may equally be because the film presents her as having managed to preserve her uncorrupted state or because it presents her as having achieved a unity or wholeness of self-determination that she once lacked. *Die Niebelungen: Kriemhild's Rache* (Lang) is closest to *Dogville* in the horrific devastation effected by the central character in response to the way she has been treated by her community. But this act is a long-planned 'atonement' (her own words to Hagen) rather than a sudden lurch into retribution, and she does not herself survive it but seems willingly to include herself in the general annihilation, as if the atonement itself must be atoned for. So the film does not force us to ask whether someone who acts inconsistently, or from a position of continuing dominant strength, or from outside and beyond those called on to atone, can be considered a person of integrity. *Dogville*, in contrast, raises the whole spectrum of questions about the nature and value of integrity in all their distinctness and force, and in this it is unique.

The narrative and thematic content of *Dogville*, its moral content and aesthetic rationale, are reflections and inflections of the question how integrity is possible. When Pasolini faced the same problem and came to the singularly honest and painful conclusion that some of his own work had failed to resolve it, he wrote a 'Repudiation' whose centre turns on a single point: 'What counts are first of all the sincerity and the necessity of what one has to say. One must not betray them in any way, least of all by remaining silent on principle' (2005: xvii). We may suppose that those responsible for creating *Dogville* arrived at a similar conclusion and recognised the validity of the point. In filmmaking no less than in the human living which *Dogville* represents, the possibility of integrity is denied in saying nothing, attempting nothing, even (or perhaps particularly) when it is 'on principle' that nothing is said, nothing attempted. If *Dogville* acts 'on principle', it is to pose problems for itself that force it to say something, attempt something. But perhaps even that is not a matter of principle and Jean-Luc Godard may be right: 'Posing problems is not a critical attitude but a natural function. When a motorist deals with traffic problems, one simply says he is driving; and Picasso paints' (1972: 222).

NOTES

1   This is one of several ways in which *Dogville* echoes Heinrich von Kleist's 'Über das Marionettentheater', a story whose central character ('Herr C.') postulates a similarly radical role for grace. For discussion of the issues as they impact on the analytic and non-analytic traditions in philosophy, see de Gaynesford (1998).

2   Knowing something of von Trier's history and his reasons for adopting radically opposed 'rules' in his earlier work does nothing to make this provocation more direct or pressing; on the contrary, it is almost impossible to attend to this history without trivialising the challenge I am referring to.

3   The parallel is as apposite here as in *La Terra Trema*, whose opening credit-sequence draws attention to the equivalence by referring to the '*Commento Parlato*' and '*Commento Musicale*'.

4   The film by Volker Schlöndorff which carries that phrase as its title, in translation (in German *Der Fangschuss*), ends with an equally abrupt departure preceded by an equally brutal execution-by-pistol of a beloved by a loved one in an equally dubious relationship.

WORKS CITED

Bresson, R. (1997) *Notes on the Cinematographer*. Trans. J. Griffin. Copenhagen: Green Integre.

Cavell, S. (1979) *The World Viewed*, enlarged edition. Cambridge, MA: Harvard University Press.

de Gaynesford, M. (1998) 'Humanism, Reflective Capacities, and Prejudice', *Angelaki*, 3, 109–16.

Eliot, T. S. (1933) *The Use of Poetry and the Use of Criticism*. Cambridge, MA: Harvard University Press.

Godard, J.-L. (1972) *Godard on Godard*. Ed. J. Narboni and T. Milne. New York: Viking Press.

Pasolini, P. P. (2005 [1972]) 'Repudiation of the Trilogy of Life', in *Heretical Empiricism* [*Empirismo eretico*], second edition. Trans. B. Lawton and L. K. Barnett, Washington: New Academia Publishing, xvii.

Dogville's 'Illustration': Ambiguous Images, Filmic Plurilingualism and Ethics

SARA FORTUNA

Even more than the other works by Lars von Trier, *Dogville* seems to stimulate a sort of irresistible, theoretical impulse, both in scholars of different disciplines and in the 'normal' audience as the several contributions, discussions and analysis about the film testify.[1] Taking this consideration as a starting point, this chapter is an attempt to confront some questions related to this issue: why does the film allow interpretations from so many diverse points of view, giving the impression of an infinite range of hermeneutical possibilities? On which formal elements of the film does this theorising impulse rely? And is the theoretical response an adequate kind of reaction to the film or, as I view it, is *Dogville*'s aim, in a paradoxical and deceptive way, rather to suggest that constructing a theory, presenting an explication of a single aspect or a few ones should give way to a form of ethical responsiveness and a sense for the totality made possible by the original plurilingualism of the film?

If one could object that all great works of art are in principle open to an infinite range of interpretations (though many critics would deny that *Dogville* is one of them), this chapter argues that in the first part of von Trier's trilogy 'USA: Land of Opportunities', this characteristic more specifically depends on the film's capacity to produce an extremely rich frame of ambiguous images like the duck-rabbit shown opposite – images where the observer can shift from one to another aspect of the image and also focus on the very phenomenon of the aspect-change.[2]

By presenting what he called a filmic experiment, von Trier forces the audience to engage not only with a very sophisticated aesthetic construction but also with an intrinsically deceptive one – one which stimulates the spectator to adopt all the possible tools at her/his disposal to try to crack the riddle. But eventually he would like to show to her/him the inanity of this attempt and the necessity to overcome this sort of 'aut-aut syndrome': because, as in the ambiguous, bistable images, the observer cannot perceive, for example, the duck and the rabbit simultaneously, but must necessarily shift from one to another or choose one and fix her/his gaze on it. In a similar way, *Dogville* creates an 'optical illusion' imbued with a hypnotic power, where the risk for the audience of concentrating on only one or a few aspects, and thereby losing the totality and the specific experience of aspect-change staged by the film, remains very high. At the same time however, the mutually self-excluding aspects within the ambiguous or multistable images proposed in the film via different formal elements (as the schematic drawing of the stage, the literary division of the story in chapters, the artificial reproduction of day and night light through the alternation of white and black background) are not to be taken as aspects between which one has to choose. After being aesthetically deceived all through the film by its ambiguous images, the audience should eventually confront the necessity of shifting its attention onto the very experience of the aspect-change, that is, to that 'tiny change of light' experienced by Grace in two crucial passages of the film – although she remains unable to overcome her manicheistic look.

The *aut-aut* syndrome staged in the film relies on a dualistic anthropological model to which the title also refers, linking together an animal – the dog, and a specifically human social construction – the *polis*, the town, and thereby creating a sort of oxymoron. There is no clear-cut border – which in my hypothesis is *Dogville's* conclusion – which separates human beings' and other species' behaviour, verbal language and different

The duck-rabbit, an ambiguous or bistable image from Ludwig Wittgenstein's *Philosophical Investigations*, II, cap.11

kinds of animal signalling; cold disembodied reason and emotional cor-poreal reactions; unconditional love and instinctive biologically-biased affection; social (and linguistic) games directed by specific rules and ethi-cal, religious and aesthetic absolute values. All of these issues are at the core of Wittgenstein's philosophical concern about language and ethics and, particularly, of his later meditations where he introduces seeing-as and aspect-change as crucial philosophical tools to understand the work of art, presenting among others the examples of bistable and multistable images and those of polysemic, ambiguous phrases such as 'time flies' typi-cal of jokes and poetry. In a similar way, Wittgenstein and von Trier seem convinced that language cannot speak directly about ethics (if it pretends to do so it rather becomes rhetoric manipulation). What language is able to do is indirectly hint at ethics by providing negative paradigms. As recent research has shown, the *Philosophical Investigations'* model of the multiplic-ity of linguistic games, which human beings play with language, could also be considered as a negative paradigm, since Wittgenstein's examples of primitive and mutually isolated linguistic games appear deprived of the

essential dimensions of the human form of life and offer an image of fragmentation and cruelly selfish orientation, which is close to the linguistic
games played by the inhabitants of Dogville staged by von Trier.

Both Wittgenstein in the first part of the *Philosophical Investigations*
and von Trier in *Dogville* sketch a Babelic scenario characterised by the
separateness of its multiple languages. They provide a 'perspicuous representation' of it, an evident illustration related to imaginary communities in which the readers/audience can perceive the heterogeneous and
mutable character of human nature in all its manifestations. Another key
point of this interpretation, which is also strongly related to Wittgenstein's
peculiar philosophical writing, is that *Dogville*'s stylistic mark is a pervasive
form of self-reflectivity: von Trier's claim that he split himself in the two
main characters, Tom and Grace, allows us to refer to the film elements
of the ironical criticism about Tom's 'illustration' via his experiment of
moral re-armament. His game involving the village and Grace as a gift
corresponds, on the level of *Dogville*, to the possibility for the audience of
becoming aware of ambiguities, contradictions and pragmatic paradoxes
which mark the experiment, at each of its steps starting from the village's
linguistic exchanges.

1. Dictum ac factum: language, performativity, ethics

There is an enigmatic motto appearing in two crucial points of the film,
dictum ac factum, a motto which, in a self-reflective perspective, can be
referred to language and performativity as two interwoven main issues of
the film. The motto is written at the entrance of an old abandoned mine
next to the village, engraved in wood. No explanation is given for it in
the film. However, in several interviews about *Dogville*, von Trier told a
story which is connected to the motto, though it is part neither of the
script nor of the film, where nobody mentions it. It is the story of a man
who kept on saying all his life that he would have dug his own mine.
Everybody laughed at his claim, but eventually he really did it and wrote
on the mine '*dictum ac factum*' ('I said it and I did it'). In these interviews,
the filmmaker also quite enigmatically affirmed that this story enriches
the film even if it is not part of it and – quite paradoxically – even if

nobody knows about it (see von Trier's interview in the DVD double edition of *Dogville*).

If we consider '*dictum ac factum*' – as I suggest we do – as a motto which helps to confront the deep ambivalence of the linguistic exchanges of the village, von Trier's claim also gives us a self-reflective clue to interpret '*dictum ac factum*' as something referring to the ethical dimension related to the link between telling and doing. That means that the ethical dimension is NOT present in the film as it rather stages a parody of ethics, a negative, distorted paradigm of it. From this perspective, could the motto '*dictum ac factum*' even resonate with the ironical, impossible promise of the filmmaker that he will be able one day, at the end of his career, confront directly that ethical dimension with which hitherto he has dealt only via negative illustrations?

'*Dictum ac factum*' as the motto of a (lazy and belated) miner has of course an immediate metaphorical connection with Tom's description as a lazy and badly prepared writer and philosopher, whose main work pretends to be 'mining' human souls: 'Tom was busy enough, even though formally speaking not yet busy with writing a piece. And if anybody found it hard to grasp what profession he was busy at he'd merely reply "mining". For although he did not blast his way through rock he blasted through what was even harder ... namely the human soul ... right into where it glistered!' In this sense '*dictum ac factum*' announces the extreme game (*factum*) Tom will play with the village in order to prove his assumption (*dictum*) that Dogville's people have a problem with receiving – a fatal experiment of moral re-armament leading to a final slaughter. When Grace, a mysterious fugitive escaping a group of gangsters who had tried to shoot her, asks him for help, Tom persuades her to remain in the village and to accept participating in his experiment by offering herself to the village as a gift. But '*dictum ac factum*' also frames the general ambiguity of every linguistic use, in which any utterance could at the same time have a referential value and be a performative act (*factum*) with diverse connotations. In Dogville the relationship between *dictum* and *factum* presents a specific anthropological interest: the performative effect at which the utterances of every person or family are aimed is to reaffirm or to reinforce her/his/its social status, identity and power within the community.

If the meaning of a sentence in most cases is its use in a specific context, as observed in *Philosophical Investigations*, the use in the linguistic game played by all the inhabitants of Dogville consists in a form of rhetoric competition. Emblematic of this kind of interaction and the manipulation which it entailed is a dialogue between Tom and Ma Ginger, the owner of an expensive shop of very kitsch objects. According to Tom, Ma Ginger rakes and hoes too much the soil into which her gooseberry bushes grow: 'I don't think it's good for the soil with all the raking and hoeing. It's the soil that gave life to us all.' Whereas Tom's intention is to direct her attention to a universal level, reminding her that the earth is a common ground for all human beings, Ma Ginger toughly reaffirms her right to treat her property as she likes: 'Don't give me any of your lip Thomas Edison Jr, I'll hoe as I darn well please!' And when her shop assistant, Gloria, agrees with Tom, the dialogue turns into a paradigmatically manipulative interaction:

> *Ma Ginger:* Yeah, well he likes eating my pies, don't you.
> *Tom:* Well they're tasty, no doubt about it.
> *Ma Ginger:* Yeah, so when it comes to hoeing who's right Tom, you or me?
> *Tom:* I'm not so sure it's that simple.

If Tom likes Ma Ginger's gooseberry pies and wants to continue to eat them he should not question her way of taking care of the gooseberry bushes. The reason she is right and Tom is wrong does not seem to depend much on some better botanic knowledge of hers or on the fact that after all her gooseberry cakes are tasty, but on the power relation between them. The manipulative and latently blackmailing pattern of this kind of linguistic exchange is more evident in another scene when Ma Ginger confronts Grace who takes a shortcut between Ma Ginger's gooseberry bushes and is stopped by a shout of the woman:

> *Grace:* Yes, I didn't see that you just raked the path, I'm sorry.
> *Ma Ginger:* It isn't that I've just raked it. The idea is that people can pass around the bushes completely. I prefer it that way as you should know.

Grace: I thought that these chains were put up to make a path between the bushes.

Ma Ginger: They were put up there to protect the bushes. It is not supposed to be a pathway.

Grace: But everyone goes this way.

Ma Ginger: Dear, that's right. They have been living here for years. You haven't been here that long.

Grace: Are you saying that I am less entitled to use the shortcut because I haven't always lived here?

Ma Ginger: No, of course not. No, I just thought it pleased you to be here, that's all. Go on, go on, it's alright.

In this case in the apparently neutral observation 'I just thought it pleased you to be here' hides the obvious implication that if Grace does not respect Ma Ginger's rule she might be forced to leave the village. Hereby the exceptional status of Grace in the village which is about to fatally deteriorate into a condition of sexual slavery is stressed once again. In their linguistic exchange with Grace the men of the village succeed in manipulating her in an even more extreme and grotesque way: Chuck's rhetorical speech about the beauty of apple cultivation; Ben's obsessive insistence that one should not 'poke fun at the freight industry'; McKay's vain exhibiting of his aesthetic taste in judging light effects which he is not able to see; Tom Edison Sr's social pride of an ex-doctor and his hypochondriac speech. All these narratives create a sort of Babel-like scenario in which the different professional jargons resonate as agonistic and isolated voices like the craftsmen's in the biblical myth about the construction of the Babel tower as a challenge to God. And although only Chuck and Ben use their speech to force Grace to accept their sexual attentions, even the child Jason verbally manipulates the woman by blackmailing her, when he demands to be spanked and threatens to tell his mother that Grace punished him, should she not accept to punish him.

The linguistic manipulation represents a specific form of violence within Dogville, which is not comparable with the physical one. Because, if the inhabitants are 'greedy as animal', as Chuck explains to Grace expressing his general pessimism towards humanity, human language cannot be compared to forms of animal signalling, whose goal is to manipulate only insofar as they are supposed to produce specific reactions. In the case of human language 'it is not that simple', as Tom observed: although verbal language could be, and is, mostly used in isolated and fragmented social games, whose aims are multiple forms of competition, it is a fact that, simultaneously, other linguistic uses, typically related to ethics and aesthetics, may be forgotten but never completely removed from consciousness. Tom's claim: 'I think there is a lot this country has forgotten. I just try and refresh folks' memory', parodically echoes the following remark in the *Philosophical Investigations*: 'The work of the philosopher consists in assembling reminders for a particular purpose' (2001: 43, §127). Tom also affirms that he can obtain his goal 'by way of illustration', whereas Wittgenstein indicates as essential for philosophical understanding the capacity to provide 'a perspicuous representation' which enables 'that understanding which consists in 'seeing connexions''(2001: 42, §122).

However, as is well known, Wittgenstein also indicates in philosophical speculation the origin of a particular form of misunderstanding and intellectual bewitchment for which philosophy must find a therapy. As observed by Stanley Cavell, the *Philosophical Investigations* stage, in highly polyphonic frames, the fight between two major voices: the voice of temptation and the voice of correctness (1989: 38). The first one is the voice of the metaphysical *hubris* in all its typical manifestations (emphasis on an isolated disembodied individual considered as a view from nowhere, on the inner as separated from the outer which is just an external sign of the inner, on a dualistic view about human freedom as opposed to biological drives, and about pure reason as opposed to instinctual feelings); the second one, the voice of correctness, seems to relate to the religious point of view from which – as Wittgenstein once told his friend Drury – all the problems of the *Philosophical Investigations* are considered. However, this ethical-religious dimension is not connected to single contents or moral teachings, but rather to a sort of philosophical conversion of the gaze which, via a perspicuous representation, eventually allows us to see the world in the right way. Dogville's moral mentor, Tom, considers his activity as something similar when he presents his spiritual struggle to refresh the village's memory and to make it confront its problem in receiving. In doing so he claims that 'we can be spiritual without singing or reading from the Bible'. And it is clear that Tom's (but also Grace's) behaviour in *Dogville* represent two (albeit very different) aspects of the metaphysical *hubris*. The next section will explore the voice of temptation, that is, the pathological traits of these philosophical figures, as directly linked to the moral degeneration of the village. It will then focus on the voice of correctness, which I identify with the multistable and plurilinguistic filmic construction that provides the possibility for an aesthetic and ethical conversion of the gaze.

2. Tom and Grace as pathological philosophical attitudes

One essential focus in *Dogville*'s illustration is related to the two main characters, Tom and Grace. However – as already observed – it would be misleading to look for their psychological unity; they can much more productively be analysed as a set of philosophical attitudes and as specific forms of separation, which these attitudes produce at different levels.[3]

If Tom is explicitly dubbed a philosopher, albeit in a quite ironic way, Grace as Dogville's improvised teacher is proud of making the children acquainted with Stoicism, which is manifestly a doctrine she first of all applies to her own life and behaviour. If metaphysics originates from an inclination of the subject to consider himself as a disembodied, neutral gaze, this typical metaphysical disposition has also a very practical and relational pendant, derived from a dualistic conceptualisation of the inner and the outer: a sceptical and desperate approach to the external world and to the internal life of other persons. If Wittgenstein's meditation proposes itself as a therapy to regain an ordinary access to language, the world and other persons, one could ask whether Grace's immediate and idealised affection for the village may not be linked to a nostalgic feeling for such a different, 'pre-philosophical' form of life. Presenting Tom and Grace as two desperate cases of the philosophical illness, von Trier seems to once again give shape to the idea explored in many of his previous films, namely that the idealist, with his/her apparently good intentions, is a most dangerous person since, by trying to impose unrealistic models upon a society, produces its worst degeneration and eventually his/her own ruin and that of the world he/she inhabits.

However, *Dogville* goes a step further, exploring the specific characters and forms that the philosophical illness and its spiritual blindness can assume. In Tom's case what is at stake is clearly *in primis* the pretence of a moral superiority, in presenting himself as mentor who is able to give a clear illustration about the community of Dogville. Tom's 'bad preparation' in proposing a moral experiment to his village is connected to the philosophical inclination to draw clear-cut distinctions where it is impossible to do so: 'Tom was a writer, at any rate by its own lights. Oh, his output as committed to paper was so far limited to the words great and small, followed by a question mark.' This poor, schematic approach to moral values echoes the *Philosophical Investigations*' claim about 'a main cause of philosophical disease – an unbalanced diet: one nourishes one's thinking with only one kind of example' (2001: 131, §593).

The use of words like 'small' referred to quantities confronts the problem which Greek philosophy called the 'sorites paradox': one is not able to decide how many grains one has to add in order to transform a small heap into a big one. And it seems that another anthropological version of this paradox consists in the impossibility to establish clear distinctions between quantitative and qualitative, relative and absolute uses of words as 'great', 'small' or 'good' and to indicate within a single use a single semantic element, separating the dimension of absolute ethical values from that of rhetoric motivations – as for instance when Tom explains to Grace that the inhabitants of Dogville are 'good, honest people' in order to persuade her to remain in the village. In particular, Tom's experiment is characterised by an intrinsic ambiguity. His game could be seen as a bistable image, in which one has to switch from the ethical aspect to the cognitive one: if the naïve assumption might be that Tom's (ethically inspired) aim should be to help the village to overcome its moral impairment, the (cognitively oriented) goal of the game seems rather to provide the specific conditions under which the village manifests in the worst form its difficulty to receive a gratuitous gift. The transformation of external conditions contributes to redirect the village's attention from Grace's aspect of a gratuitous gift to her being a fugitive who needs to hide in the village, and whose permanence could be materially exploited, demanding for it an increasing price. Tom seems to oscillate between these extremes, an oscillation which one should not interpret from a psychological point of view as a sign of a disturbed, inconsistent mind, but rather as various aspects of a typically philosophical problem.

As a matter of fact, Tom never identifies Dogville's ethical problem as one which could affect him too. He mostly acts as an external agent, a neutral viewer, and never considers this position as the source of a specific ethical blindness. One should not forget that Dogville indeed succeeds in accepting Grace as a gift as it showed in the scenes of the village's decision to allow her to stay during the national celebration of the Fourth of July. This ethical climax is summarised by the narrator's voice: 'The period of spring and early summer proved a happy one for Grace. Martha rang the hours conducting her through the day. So she could serve as eyes for McKay, a mother for Ben, friend for Vera and brains for Bill...' If the game goes on after the early successful result this means that Tom/von Trier wants rather to show that the village, despite a previous deceptive acceptance, is not able to receive a gratuitous gift in a stable and durable way. A severe lack of concentration on his own ethical problem seems to depend on the obsessive concentration on the game Tom/von Trier wants to play and win with *Dogville*. Also typical of a classical philosophical attitude is Tom's sublimation of bodily drives and his detachment from a personal experience in which he could manifest his own individual feelings (as his love for Grace whose 'actualisation' is constantly postponed with intellectual excuses throughout the film).

The case of Grace as an expression of a philosophical inclination is obviously much more complicated and it is not surprising that von Trier claimed in an interview that the character of Grace turned him into a feminist (see the interviews in the DVD double edition of *Dogville* and the interview with the director in this volume). This, however, must not be interpreted in a positive sense. The complexity of Grace and the unexpected final development, in which she shifts from the victim character to that of the self-avenger, allows one to reconsider retrospectively the female characters of von Trier's previous films (Bess in *Breaking the Waves* and Selma in *Dancer in the Dark*), and to question the frequent interpretations according to which the filmmaker would aim at presenting his female victims as paradigmatic positive examples. Grace, as a bistable-image of victim and self-avenger, is even a less positive (though surely more interesting) example than the others. Grace, as a philosopher with a preference for Stoicism, has also a much deeper awareness than Tom that philosophy, or rather, and more generally, intellectual activity, is connected with an arrogant disposition, and that a spiritual exercise in modesty is the best tool against it. As narcissism seems to be for Grace one of the multiple forms that arrogance can assume, she avoids in her interaction with Dogville to refer to herself, to her past life, privileges and social status. In doing so, Grace also adopts a classical female model which prescribes altruism to women, whereas her compassion for the inhabitants' moral weakness is an expression of both an ethical-religious attitude and a typical feminine behaviour.

Grace-as-philosopher participating in Tom's experiment will give herself as a gift to Dogville trying to accept herself via an ideal kind of relationship. Her verbal communication pretends to be independent from her concrete situation: she denies that what she does and tells has, as its aim, to convince the village to like her; at the same time it is clear that despite her claim (inspired by the typical philosophical illusion that meaning could entirely depend on the intention of the speaker, no matter what the contextual conditions are), this is not true. The meaning of her altruistic behaviour and speeches, as little Jason maliciously reveals to her, is inevitably interpreted as an attempt to be liked by the village for a specific reason: 'You want people to like you, so you don't have to go away.'

Another most philosophical trait in Grace's attitude (but also rather familiar to the cultural model of feminine abnegation) is the detachment from her bodily dimension, her emotions, preferences, desires. When she is sexually abused by Chuck, she does not even attempt to react physically; her only form of defence consisting in the repetition of the words: 'Please. Stop it. Please, please, please, please, don't, please, please. Please look at me. Look at me, talk to me. We're friends. You are my family.' And these pathetic, moving words sound surprisingly ineffective, as if she did not trust them herself and as if her look on the village originated from an external position. Even her love for Tom is expressed in a neutral way, as if she were speaking about someone else.

The filmmaker sketches Grace's character as a set of bistable images and shifts the audience's gaze. In a first bistable image we see the philosophical aspect of detachment as characterised by pure will and rational control and then the other aspect, a sort of passive, animal, attitude overwhelming the woman after the rape: 'It was not Grace's pride that kept her going during the days when fall came and the trees were losing their leaves but more of the trance-like state that descends on animals, whose lives are threatened, a state in which the body reacts mechanically.' This aspect also includes the perspective of the village: while Grace is stuck in the traumatic condition of a sexual slave, her humanity is removed in the inhabitants' perception, as observed by the voiceover: 'the harassments in bed did not have to be kept so secret anymore because they couldn't really be compared to a sexual act. They were embarrassing the way it is when a hillbilly has his way with a cow, but no more than that'. In another bistable image we shift from the aspect of the victim's arrogance to that of the self-avenger. Grace's first kind of arrogance (which prompts her father's reproaches to her) consists in refusing to apply to others the same high moral standards by which she would judge herself, and in justifying the worst ethical behaviour with the motivation that the responsible are simply unable to act in a different way.

However, a second and more radical form of arrogance is the refusal to consider her own position as based on concrete conditions in any significant way (the Stoic attitude). In this sense the development of the story punishes her with a ferocious *contrapasso* reducing her to a form of animality. And nevertheless Grace also stubbornly persists in her inability to recognise this dimension when we eventually see her as an implacable self-avenger. In the final scenes she decides that the gangsters must eliminate the village, refusing his father's suggestion to just shoot the dog as an instructive example for the inhabitants: here she gives a universalistic motivation for her decision: 'What they had done was not good enough. And if one had the power to put it to rights, it was one's duty to do so for the sake of the other towns. For the sake of humanity. And not least for the sake of the human being that was Grace herself.' Hypocrisy clearly resonates in these words as Grace refuses once again to abandon her neutral philosophical attitude and, instead, considers herself just like any other human being she wants to protect. In the end, both Tom's and Grace's arrogant characters prove to be very consistent in their interaction with the community and with each other. Whereas Tom's last words about his mission as a moral writer as an implicit reason to be spared from the slaughter constitute his last attempt at manipulating Grace, her own final speech proves that she still remains split, detached from her bodily and emotional reactions. She pretends to be a mere disembodied moral instance, which eventually decides that Dogville does not after all reach the minimal moral standards and therefore has to be eliminated for the sake of humanity.

Obviously everyone can see that the real motivation behind her decision is to take vengeance for all she had to suffer in Dogville and one must agree with Slavoj Žižek's remark that, in expressing this resentment and condemning the village to death, Grace becomes like its inhabitants and is eventually in the right condition for being accepted by them (2009: 286). However, she still finds it hard or even impossible to admit this fact, and pretends, like Tom, that she is moved by a universal motivation. Hereby she manifests once more the character of an incurable philosopher, unable to assume a concrete, situated point of view and to recognise her negative feelings as peculiar of a common human condition. Even if the animal dimension in her seems in the end to prevail, as it is symbolically shown in Grace's final warm farewell from the dog Moses, the only survivor in the village, this fact is far from representing a solution for the moral problem opened by Dogville's game. Until its last paradoxical sentence, *Dogville's* script playfully proposes again and again the dualistic temptation of an impossible *aut-aut* about human experience confronting the audience with an apparently aporetic end: 'Whether Grace left Dogville or on the contrary Dogville had left her and the world in general is a question of a more artful nature that few would benefit from by asking and even fewer by providing an answer. And nor indeed will it be answered here!'

3. Filmic multi-aspectuality and ethical seeing-as

In a recent article Carlo Ginzburg compares his methodology with a sort of 'imbecile approach': 'You have heard perhaps of the Chinese proverb

… which says: "When a finger points to the moon, the imbecile looks at the finger". I'm one of those imbeciles' (2010: 150–1). I suggest adopting this approach in order to confront *Dogville* from an aesthetic point of view and want to argue that this is the only way to understand the complex riddle posed by the film. To apply the imbecile strategy here means to focus our attention on the original plurilinguistic form of the film and on a peculiar tension between the two main strategies which this filmic plurilingualism adopts. This move implies taking seriously the clearly self-reflective considerations about Tom's strategy: 'To illustrate the human problem to receive, Tom made diligent use of his technique of lashing out somewhat haphazardly in all directions.' Transposed to *Dogville* this claim refers to its hybrid form. But what in this illustration enables it to produce in the audience an aesthetic awareness connected with a sense for the ethical dimension? In order to attempt to answer this point and to grasp the core of *Dogville's* peculiar filmic invention, it could be useful to go back to Wittgenstein's definition of perspicuous representation in *Philosophical Investigations*:

> A main source of our failure to understand is that we do not *command a clear view* of the use of our words. – Our grammar is lacking in this sort of perspicuity. A perspicuous representation produces just that understanding which consists in 'seeing connections'. Hence the importance of finding and inventing *intermediate cases*. (2001: 42, §122)

Dogville's aesthetics applies this view creating intermediate positions: between theatre and film first of all. Von Trier mentioned Brecht's theatrical technique of the *Verfremdungseffekt* as one of his sources of inspiration, but he is clearly aiming at something much more complicated or even contradictory – something which could be analysed by considering the classical antinomy in the interpretation of the nature of cinema and the semiotic solution which Roman Jacobson gave to the antinomy. The Russian linguist draws on St Augustine's distinction between *res* and *signum* and the semiotic function of specific objects' uses: 'It is precisely things (visual and auditory), transformed into signs, that are the specific material of cinematic art' (1987: 459). He also highlights the perspectival variety of this semiotic transformation: 'Film works with manifold fragments of time and space likewise varied. It changes their proportions and juxtaposes them in terms of contiguity or similarity and contrast; that is, it takes the path of metonymy or metaphor (two fundamental kinds of cinematic structure)' (1987: 460). As is well known, for Jacobson metaphor and metonymy are the two organising principles of every symbolic construction, where, however, only one principle always prevails at a time. Commenting on the enormous popularity of this distinction, Luisa Muraro observes that Jacobson also stresses the intrinsic rivalry between the two principles, their being 'almost enemies to each other' (2004: 51). She also reminds us that this tension had been mostly neglected by theorists, who reduced every symbolic process to the metaphoric construction. Exploring the reasons for the cultural prevailing of the metaphor, Muraro indicates the loss related to the philosophical attitude of the bodily roots of the human experience, and the need of transcending the body shared by philosophy and art in their metaphorical drive. In her short but seminal work, Muraro explicitly endorses a feminist perspective as a counter-thinking which recovers the metonymic principle and puts it at the core of its activity via a reflection intermingled with witty embodied narratives.

One could say that, in *Dogville*, von Trier takes seriously the enmity between metaphor and metonymy, shaping his filmic construction so as to reflect a tension which somewhat corresponds to that between the two voices, of temptation and correctness (which Stanley Cavell also reads in *Philosophical Investigations*). On the one hand, the numerous analogical clues 'haphazardly' disseminated in the script represent the metaphoric technique: this contagiously affects the interpreters of the film, who are forced to adopt all possible theories and hermeneutic models to confront the film's complexity – which is obviously also the case of my contribution. On the other, the set of the little village is highly metonymical: a sort of play-board drawn with white chalk on a dark floor and a minimalistic scenario in which the actors interact with invisible objects as handles, bushes, and where landscapes and bodily movements are accompanied by naturalistic sounds of opening doors and windows. The *pars pro toto* principle realised through the plurilinguistic or rather plurisemiotic frame of the filmic experiment gives access to the ethical dimension in very specific metonymic forms: through the absence of borders and walls in the town set sketched as an opened totality, through the artificial landscape background and the imperfect framing of the manual camera slowly and gently approaching the visages and their mimic expressions. The different spaces sketched on the floor (the houses of the different family), those bi-dimensional figures deprived of depth, also mirror the egoistic fragmentation and ambiguity of linguistic games staged in the script.

The audience is confronted with the fact that a very essential and schematic stage is sufficient to create deep involvement in the actions of the characters, as if they had occurred in a normal, 'complete', naturalistic context. Nevertheless the audience is also forced to constantly shift from a naïve attitude to a reflective one, which enables it to access to the formal level of the film. The multiple filmic techniques make the observers aware of the ethical sense of the story and allow them to experience the shift between sympathy and insensibility, violence and fragility, bodily instincts and Stoic detachment, claims and beliefs, verbal statements and practical deeds. The aesthetic mastery of a complex totality and its internal tensions corresponds to a very specific ethical answer. Assuming the cultural and philosophical legacy of an art form like cinema, whose thinking potential is embodied in the movement and rhythm of its images, von Trier suggests that the only approach to the Babel-like scenarios of multiple and fragmented linguistic practices in mutual competition is a filmic plurilingualism, that is, its creation of a totality which overcomes the isolation of the different linguistic games, and takes into account the intermediate, in-between condition of the intrinsically mutable human experience.

Like Wittgenstein, von Trier seems to believe that one cannot talk about ethics and that one can only give examples, typically aesthetic illustrations of ethical problems. All the 'ethical moments' in *Dogville* are imbued with a sort of ineffability, the scenes of friendship and happiness are mute, we are not able to listen to the dialogues. When Grace has already been abused by all the inhabitant of the village and Tom suggests that she explains to the inhabitants what they did, we can just see her from the distance but cannot hear her words. The ethical dimension is here exhibited in Grace's angelic and suffering physiognomy, in her body humiliated by a thick chain put around her neck, her movements burdened by the heavy wheel which she is forced to drag. And exactly in the moment in which we deepen our compassionate attention into this metonymic frame, the metaphorical aspect starts to interfere with it, making us wonder about the weird *contrapasso* inflicted upon Grace. The rudimentary tool which is the cause of her imprisonment was albeit indirectly built though her intellectual aid to Bill, and it is a wheel, the first of the technical inventions of humanity, symbol of movement and progress.[4] In that context it becomes for Grace an instrument of slavery, and one cannot but link this metaphorical clue to other negative references to technology in the film, the first of which is Tom's very name: Thomas Edison was a prolific American inventor, whose technical devices strongly affected the Western process of industrialisation as well as its scientific methodology. But this theoretical attempt to understand the film's alleged metaphorical message about technology and politics distracts us from our compassionate approach to Grace's troubles, although we entertain the inevitable illusion that our understanding could be a sort of constructive substitute of compassion.

If the metonymic and the metaphoric strategies are the two organising axes of *Dogville*, and if it is true that their tensions shape a specific bistable image through which von Trier confronts the paradox of the human condition, it would be misleading to see the unexpected finale of the film as a move back to reality through an ideological and critical representation of American society. The link between the pictures showing Americans affected by the Great Depression and the bombastic rhythm of David Bowie's 'Young Americans' stages again a tension with a double movement. The quick flow on the screen of so many persons, their intense mimic expression, the limited access we have to their lives and world, stimulate our imagination and desire of a deeper, longer and silent contemplation. This is in contrast with the mysterious ambivalence of Bowie's song, in which an absolute despair lurks behind its narcissistic vitality, thus stimulating again in the audience the metaphoric drive to decipher the message, the sense of the weird association of photographs and song.

So *Dogville* takes its leave from the audience with a last bistable image, whose aspects are in dialogue with the previous ones and – as suggested also in some contributions of this volume – with all von Trier's films and with the work of other filmmakers. From this perspective it is clear that perceiving these aspects is but a first step; the most decisive one will concern our decision about which, amongst them, we will focus our attention on, and what we will do with them: the ethical, religious (metonymic) inclination of Lars von Trier would suggest that we take the path of modesty or even of authentic idiocy, whereas his metaphysical (metaphoric) orientation, his aesthetic *hubris* of a genial artist would force him (and us) on the path of creative arrogance. The result is a paradigmatic representation of internal tensions which are not characteristic of a single exceptional individual, but rather enable us to understand more about a crucial paradoxical trait of the human condition.

NOTES

1   See the Preface to this volume. I would like to thank the students who attended my courses in Philosophy of Language at the University of Rome 'La Sapienza' in the Summer Semester 2005 and those of the Masters in Philosophical Counseling at the Universities of Cagliari, Pisa and Naples who took part in my workshop in Castiglioncello in September 2006 for their comments and the passionate discussions on *Dogville*.

2   Aspect-change is the expression used by Ludwig Wittgenstein to indicate the shift from one aspect to another in bistable or multistable images. This phenomenon is also defined as 'seeing-as'. The definition refers to the voluntary character of the aspect-shift: one can for instance follow the indication to see something now as x, now as y. In my analysis of *Dogville* I will use aspect-change, seeing–as, perception of aspects in this Wittgensteinian sense.

3   See Dell'Aversano's and de Gaynesford's chapters in this volume.

4   I want to thank Roberta Pasquarè who drew my attention on the metaphorical richness of the wheel in connection to this scene.

WORKS CITED

Cavell, S. (1989) 'Declining Decline', in *This New Yet Unapproachable America. Lectures after Emerson after Wittgenstein.* Albuquerque: Living Batch Press, 29–79.

Ginzburg, C. (2010) 'Dante's Blind spot (Inferno XV–XVII)', in S. Fortuna, M. Gragnolati and J. Trabant (eds) *Dante's Plurilingualism: Authority, Vulgarization, Subjectivity'.* Oxford: Legenda, 150–63.

Jakobson, R. (1987 [1933]) 'Is the Film in Decline?', in K. Pomorska and S. Rudy (eds) Cambridge, MA: Harvard University Press, 458–65.

Muraro, L. (2004 [1981]) *Maglia o uncinetto: Racconto linguistico-politico sull'inimicizia tra metafora e metonimia.* Roma: manifesto libri.

Wittgenstein, L. (2001 [1953]) *Philosophical Investigations.* Oxford: Blackwell.

Žižek, S. (2009) 'Zorn und Ressentiment', in M. Jongen, S. van Tuinen and K. Hemesoet (eds) *Die Vermessung des Ungeheuren.* München: Fink, 277–88.

The *Dekalog* Interview: Lars von Trier

INTERVIEWERS: SARA FORTUNA & LAURA SCURIATTI[1]

You often said that theoretical essays on your films have never been of any use for you, and we are aware of that. Is it the same for the reaction of the audience? Do you ever try and imagine the point of view of the spectators?

No, actually. I usually say that I am my own audience, in the sense that I make films as I would like to see them as audience. I think with films you can try and please yourself and thereby please others. I think it is very difficult to have any idea of what an audience would think. Also I think it is very 'Hollywood' to think of an audience. I do not think of an audience. What we normally do is some testing, but that is only to see if the storyline is understandable. We do not have the kind of tests where we ask people: 'Did you like this and this? When were you bored during the film?'

It is a very egocentric thing for me to make a film. The only thing I can see is myself, what my taste is, and if I can be moved by this film – and if I can, maybe others could be too. I do not write for other people, I can't.

In *Epidemic* you say that a film should be like 'a stone in your shoe'. Of course you say it within the film as a character, but if you make films for yourself, is that what you are trying to do to yourself, to disturb yourself?

Yes, we had a long discussion here when I made *Antichrist*, and I found out that all the films I make have much to do with my mother [laughs and sighs] ... much more than I would like to, you know ... In every film I try to take the opposite point of view of what would have been hers, and the opposite point of view of my own too. *Dogville*, for example, is a film about revenge – at least for me that's the starting point. And I think that revenge is the least usable action. Also, I was taught in my childhood that revenge was a forbidden thing. For example, that the trial system is when the state steps in so that there should not be any kind of revenge, so that the trial does not become a personal revenge. So this film is about an act of revenge, and I as a spectator don't buy it, you know it's terrible – the ending of the film. But I know that people who see it have a tendency to say 'Ok, but they deserved it', but that's not how I see it.

Why don't you 'buy' it?

You know, with this film I am trying to defend the action of revenge, in the same way as I was trying in *Breaking the Waves*, to defend that kind of religion which Bess has, and ultimately in different films I am trying to defend different points of view that are not my own.

Nor your mother's point of view?

No, no! Actually I am finding out all the time that if I want to provoke one person, that's my mother! [Laughs] ... even though she's been dead for ... hmm ... twenty years... But it's ridiculous and I hate that she could be so influential ... and the older you get, unfortunately, the more you get back to your mother's or your father's point of view, even though when you are young you make a detour, but then you have a tendency to come back to that and you hear yourself say exactly the same things to your children that your parents told you.

And the first time you hear that, you are really shocked and think 'Oh shit, did I really say that?!', but I think that there is a biological explanation for that. If you are a young animal you have to be thrown out of home and do something your own way, and then you go around being a rebel for some time and then you have a family and go back to your traditions. Like amongst animals, when the mother chases away the little kittens, they have to find a new territory, and when they have a new territory, they go through this rebel-phase and then come back – it makes perfect sense.

So do you think that the story of the struggle between Grace and her father in *Dogville* and *Manderlay* can be read in that way? Is that what is it about?

Yeah, that's kind of about it… The father is a very sensible man, strangely enough … even though he represents evil, so to say, because he is a gangster, but he seems very sympathetic in life … [laughs] you know, he only wants to kill the dog, because it usually helps…

We are very curious about the trilogy, which is yet unfinished. Of course, after the election of Obama we thought that perhaps your 'American imaginary', as you called it, might have changed, and our question would be about how, and if, you are still thinking about making the third part of the trilogy

Yes, that's a very good question. But still, you know, even if now there is Obama, compared to my political views, America is still very right-wing. Of course, Obama's election is something that you would not have guessed… Just a few years ago nobody would have guessed it. It was sudden, it went much faster than you expected… It is very interesting … and this health reform … it will be very interesting to see how it goes, because, as I see it, the core of the whole soul of America is that you pay yourself for things, that you have the freedom to choose a hospital – if you have the money you are free to choose. I think that's a radical change…

We also have a question about Obama's rethinking of the issue of race and how it could be related to *Manderlay*, or even to the third part of the trilogy.

Yes, yes, I am still thinking about it... My problem is that at the time I thought it was very mature to make films that look like each other, but they are difficult to sell. I am still looking for number three, but I can't just make it as a 'number three': it has to have a value of its own... Let's see what happens...

What interests us about the USA trilogy, as well as in *Dear Wendy*, which you wrote for Thomas Vintenberg, is the fact that they represent not just an imaginary America, but also small communities which seem to be very smoothly set up, and suddenly a foreigner/ stranger arrives and it's a challenge which these communities cannot withstand: they just fall apart, ethically, morally. Is this also a reflection on xenophobia and fear of immigration in general? Do you also want to offer, through these films, a political solution?

Dramatically it is a cliché: somebody comes from the outside and kind of uncovers the faults within a community, but my idea about *Dogville* is that there is a lot of talk about a gift in the beginning, and that it was interesting to give this township a gift of a person with good intentions. The whole thing was much inspired by the song by Bertold Brecht, 'Jenny Räubertochter', which was a very good opening for me because the whole idea of revenge was very strong... I am very proud of *Dogville*. It is a very long film and has a long script but it really wrote itself, and was because what you do when you are writing is to take your whole personality and put it into the characters – anyway, that's how I do it – and then it becomes very easy to write. And it was indeed a very joyful script to write. You could say that the major fault about the film – if that's a fault – is that Grace is too good to be true. She never tries to defend herself during the film ... but eventually it is like in the Old Testament. She even kills the children, but not the dog. The whole idea when you work with stuff like that is that you do not think too much, otherwise you will be stuck all the time.

Perhaps one could say that, instead that you think through filming...

Yes, but it is a classical film in the sense that it moves along. It is not so classical in terms of set, of course... The set was so unusual... It is a long film but you can follow the story quite easily. But I like very much that it is so long – And all these words... We took about a third of the words out: they talk like hell!

Did you do that together with the actors?

No, I did that afterwards. We filmed the whole script but the voiceovers were extremely long. I wrote it in Danish and then it was translated, and we thought it sounded very English, and then John Hurt came and told us 'You can't say that, that's not English!', so we had to twist it around again...

Concerning the technical aspects of the film, we read in an interview with Stig Bjørkmann that for every thought you try to find an *ad hoc* technical solution, otherwise you would find it difficult to express that thought, or maybe even having that thought... This made us think about the question of temporality in the film: the idea that you are free, that at any moment things could have been different in the story. Did you explicitly conceive the chapter structure as an expression of the thought that at any moment, these cuts in the story express the fact of contingency, of freedom, in the sense that Grace has the possibility to act differently, but she fails?

Yes, she has lots of possibilities to do things differently. For example she could have told everybody about the rapes. Had she said something, for example about the first offence, the village would have had the opportunity of doing something to themselves, but since she is such a silent person, who just wants to be all good and not to bow down to the level where she can discuss what happened to her, then this is something that could have occurred to her anywhere in the world, because she does not give the village an opportunity to change, because she does not change.

Yes, and is it obtained through the division in chapters, which we find also in *Antichrist*? Do these cuts between chapters aim at conveying the idea of the possibility of freedom?

The chapter structure comes to me from children's stories, for example *Winnie the Pooh*: there you have at the beginning of each chapter a summary of what happens within it. This is what I do. This creates a little excitement because you know that this and that is going to happen but you do not know how it is going to happen. I just saw again the film *In Cold Blood* – have you seen it? It is a film noir about a series of murders, based on the novel by Truman Capote.

I was very inspired by that when I made *Dancer in the Dark*. Throughout the film you know what's going to happen but you don't see it until the end. It is extremely efficient as a dramatic tool, the fact that they tell you from the beginning what's going to happen but not how and when. It is like a magnet for your interest, because you have the overall structure but you become interested in the little details, because you do not have to tell the story. It is a very interesting thing that you don't work very much with this method today...

This is also a technique that early novelists used.

Yes, in fact my inspiration came mostly from *Barry Lyndon*; there are a few films that I really really like, and this is one of them. With a very strange cast... [laughs]

Did the very famous scene apparently shot only with candlelight inspire you for your reflection on light in *Dogville* and *Manderlay*?

I don't know. They claimed that they filmed only by candlelight, but I do not believe it is really true. I really struggle with light; lights are difficult. I am not very fond of the way in which we used light in *Antichrist*. Some of the monumental stuff is fine and stylised, but the rest of the film ... hmm ... I would like to be able to do a realistic film! And that's why we use these small video cameras, so we do not have to put up many lamps here and there, and get lots of shadows … natural light is beautiful, but I do not know how to achieve it.

Another question about Grace. Is she also a moral radical? Is she too pure and then falls prey to a dark side?

It seems she wasn't so pure after all … she is pure and good only in principle, and this is difficult. That's why she turns to revenge in the end. Her attempt to be good in this way is kind of unnatural; she is an idealist – and this in my films was always doomed to failure. Her idealism collides with the way of life of a town which, one can imagine, has lived quite well before her arrival.

This is a sort of joke rather than a proper question. A small group of Germans emigrated to South America in the middle of the twentieth century and decided to found New Königsberg, a sort of 'Kantsville' inspired by the principles of Immanuel Kant's philosophy. How would a 'Vontrierville' look like?

This is what I am trying not to think about. This is why I make films; but of course I have my emotions and my mothers' beliefs … the poor people who should live in this town would be very frustrated and unhappy. It is like when, with one of my boys, we saw a film about the environment and global warming, and at the end of the film he turned to me and asked: 'But where is the good news?' and I had to answer: 'There is no good news.' This would be very much like 'Vontrierville': NO GOOD NEWS! I think that what I can do is ask some questions. When you have the characters the film writes itself. *Dogville* is very mechanical in the way in which it proceeds.

Dogville **and** *Manderlay* **contain reflections on painting, photography, theatre… We were also very intrigued that 'Manderley' is also the name of the house featuring in Daphne du Maurier's** *Rebecca*, **filmed by Hitchcock: what are your figures of reference in literature and painting? And why** *Rebecca*? **Were you thinking about the novel or about Hitchcock?**

Oh, definitely Hitchcock. The style of the film was inspired by the Royal Shakespeare Company's staging of Dickens' *Nicholas Nickleby*. I found this very theatrical way of staging very interesting. Theatre has a special quality, also because it is so unusual to see theatre on TV. One listens to the words in a different way, because you know that the words are not just there to sound naturalistic, to form a naturalistic image: they are there for another purpose also. As it is obvious with *Dogville* I like words and I like the idea that the voiceover is sarcastic towards what happens in the film, because it brings in it another layer that has more to do with literature…

…and why *Rebecca*, why Hitchcock?

I wouldn't say that *Rebecca* is a favourite film of mine, but I have seen it many times, also as a child, and I was very scared. But it is difficult to answer because when it is a long time since you have shot the film one tends to think more about the funny things that happened during the shooting rather than of the film itself… The real creation for me happened during scriptwriting, and it wasn't difficult to write at all. I was a little inspired by Steinbeck and Hemingway. My America is somewhere where I have never been, so it is 'Lars von Trier's America'.

Why are you so interested in arrogance?

The story in all my films is more or less always the same: an idealist comes in and has in mind ideas about how society should work and be happy together and then he comes and tries to force his ideas on people without having really any idea of what he is doing which is something – I think – we see a lot of especially when you look at Africa today. It's really screwed because all these colonies and all this kind of people that are trying to force their ways of life on them and they are really screwed because somehow one has really to develop things inside of himself (in order to be able to understand) and reading books and stuff it is good, but the best teaching is when you have the idea yourself.

But the arrogant in your films are also hypocrite; what they really want is to have power. Let's take Tom in *Dogville* who pretends to be able to help the village in the moral rearming but at the same time wants to humiliate his friend in the chess game... And then it is clear that his programme of moral rearming cannot work...

Yes, Tom is really unsympathetic. I guess it is also a sort of self-portrait...

Would you consider a possible interpretation of *Antichrist* that the evil there is the result of the interaction of both man and women, that is, of the context in which they move and that they produce?

I rather would say that *Antichrist* has to do with my personal attitude, that it is the expression of my lack of believing that someone could have created the world. I think it's so mean. Life and how the world is put together. I tried to become a Catholic but then I come back to what my parents were: they were very anti-religious. Their religion was to be anti-religious.

But religion could also be something a-confessional, not related to the official churches but rather to the affective dimension. To compassion, for example...

Well, compassion is something that I have thought about a lot. The Danish word for 'compassion' – *medfølelse* – also means 'to feel together'. Compassion demands that you are able to feel the same. If I have anxiety and some people feel the same anxieties as me I understand them completely and really feel with them, but for people who have no anxieties and do not share them with me ... it's much more difficult. Compassion demands that you are able to feel the same thing.

But is it not a question of degree? To some degree everyone knows anxiety...

Yes, but it is not fair because you have the tendency to project your feelings onto others. If you feel something in your body, something that really hurts, then it is not fair to all other forms of hurts you don't know about to identify them with yours. To feel with somebody is something I just thought about a lot ... it's really impossible. And no good measurement is possible because it's really difficult to measure feelings in other people.

We see your point, but in *Antichrist* both figures lost their child: is this not a good basis for compassion?

Yes, there could be compassion. But originally in *Antichrist* the male character was much tougher, because this therapy is very tough and the way he uses the therapy is much tougher than as it is now in the film; so in the script he became so unsympathetic that eventually you really wanted to kill him all the time. The therapy he adopts is really hard and while for example in the film he embraces her when she is crying after her child's death, in the original script she tries to embrace him, but he refuses and answers: 'It is not what you need right now.' Because that is what a therapist in a normal therapy session would have said: 'Stay in the situation and don't try to get out of it and tell me what is happening instead of embracing as a way to skip away.' We changed a lot the script because if we had followed the scheme of a real therapy it would have been much harder.

And why did you decide to change it?

It became uninteresting somehow, because normal people don't know this form of therapy and then if there had been no feelings and no love at every point between the two main figures I don't think it would have worked. I can understand it because I went through it; I have done such therapy and I know that when psychologists are very hard they really mean well. But it is not understandable if you just listen to them telling these things in a film.

This brings us to another question. In many of your films you seem to reflect on the idea that relations among people are ruled by power struggles and authority, and that many figures cannot come to terms

with that. And at the same time both the story and the form, the way your films are presented, seem to reflect this element. There are always many rules and at times the films are like games ... what is the meaning of these rules? Also, before you said you want to make very realistic films. Is it the case for you then, that rules which seem very artificial ultimately become instruments to create something which is not artificial?

Well, as you know, civilisation consists of rules and very artificial ones too. So I want to kill you, but I don't kill you for example, because it would be very impractical if people ran around killing each other. Maybe the whole thing comes from the fact that I have imposed on myself a very strict self-discipline, which I lacked in my childhood. To put it very naively: as there was not much discipline during my childhood, I had to bring it in myself. I just made an interview in my childhood home and it was extremely unpleasant to go there. As a child I already had OCD (obsessive compulsive disorders) and I had to develop some rituals in order for the world not to go under – many rituals, magical rituals, very precise in order for the world not to collapse.

So it was a way to give shape to the world?

Maybe, but even though it was magic and not a game but something childish: you really felt that you saved the world. And so are the characters in my films: because they do something they really think is good for the world. But actually, just because you do something it doesn't mean that what you did is necessarily good. But they are like me and believe very much in themselves and in what they bring into the world. So on the one hand they are scared – and I was a very scared child – but on the other hand they (and I) had the feeling that when the world did not collapse then they should have some credit for it ... somehow. Because you did not know that I was saving also your world at that time. And you know when you are trying to be good – as you can see in my films – you can be very mean and you can do very stupid things... [long pause] I'm a pessimist ... I really am.

A pessimist about the world, but you are not pessimistic about your art, are you?

No, that's right. And if you ask me about religion, when I see one of my favourite films I come close to a kind of religious feeling. It's really interesting ... cinema is just a medium like every other media but for me it's really religious: little scenes from Tarkovsky's films, very little ones ... I'm sure he had not thought a lot about them, but ... I appreciate them so much...

So probably also your free childhood had a role in your art. If you had to recreate rules which you imposed on yourself only later, that was important for your creativity's development, wasn't it? So maybe your mother was right, don't you think?

Yes, but I still have ... I have a very problematic relationship with my mother. Not with my father. But my mother for me was like the power. She was a feminist, she was a leader of the Danish feminist movement for some years. And she was part of the Danish Resistance movement during the war. She was close to getting killed, so she was a hero.

And was she an artist?

Not at all. She was a civil servant. She worked in a ministry and so did my father.

After *Antichrist* came out, a film of yours was once more accused to be misogynistic. How do you answer to this criticism?

I discussed with journalists and I said: 'But why should I have done ten films about women if I hated them? It would have been a little bit of a waste of time.'

One could reply: 'Because you are obsessed by them.'

Yes, of course if you want to be very mean with them, but it would also have been a waste of time for me. I think that it is for me a little bit like for Bergman, you know he had this puppet theatre. And of course I also create my film characters inspired by the persons I met and it is also important what sex they have, but I could have as well just turned it around.

In an interview about *Dogville* you said that while making this film you became a feminist. Of course it was a joke but nevertheless this statement proved to be true also of your following film *The Boss of it All* where we find a very positive female character, a lawyer and an idealist, an ironic and strong person, who is determined to win her battle. So are you really a feminist like your mother?

Yes, I think so [deep sigh]. But my mother was also very much against quotas, the fact that women should be equally represented in public employment etc., because to her it was important that people were judged for what they could do. And she found it degrading that women should not be considered for their real merits and talents... So probably I'm a feminist. But I don't want to be...

Why don't you want to be feminist? Would it not be great?

Well, because I have problems with women. I'm terrible. It has also been very difficult to have relationships with women. When I was a boy I read a lot of Strindberg and I loved this struggle between men and women. I had this very romantic longing for a very strong struggle between the sexes. And everybody talks about Strindberg's hate for women but he also was focusing on women in all his literary life. And he had been influenced by Nietzsche and he had this feeling that a man should be strong; but he was not strong he was just childish, like me. So he had this romantic idea. And you know, he could not really fight, he was too small. I have always been very tiny too, and I have never fought with anybody. I just got knocked down a couple of times. I feel I'm not a good man, really.

So I'm fighting my feminism a little bit because it is difficult to be weak and not a real man and to have to interact with strong women.

However what is interesting is that I became such a relatively good director of female actors. While in your ordinary life there are so many feelings and you get easily irritated etc., it is different in a situation in which you are really focused on what you obtain by doing the film. In these cases I become much better, very patient. I want to work together with an actress under the best condition, I praise a lot and we discuss for a long time and try to figure out how we could come closer to a goal … we just have normally a very good relation and contact.

Sometimes as a female spectator it is impossible not to feel puzzled, oppressed and angry about the female figures in your films. And we discussed some of the reasons for example in *Dogville*. If we were to play a little game in which you become a woman watching your films, would you be able to say why a woman would feel like that?

I would probably hate it, but it depends also, if I looked at the films superficially I think I would hate them. But I think that as a woman I would also understand that it is a kind of little game. That is that I use female characters to carry a specific part of me in the film. And I think that the characters are very human or I'm trying to make them very human, whereas all my male characters are idiots, more or less. They are very stupid… They are always a disaster… The male characters don't get anywhere, because they are obsessed by their projects. Even in *The Idiots* if anyone gets anywhere that is Karen, who, you know, is one of the main characters in the film. So this is a very stereotyped frame.[2]

Do you have your own idea about sadomasochism?

The interesting thing is: who is in command, who has the command of the game, and I think it is the masochist, which is illogical. And it is quite easy to understand where all that is coming from: in Christianity there is so much self-destruction.

Thank you so much for your time and this extremely interesting conversation.

NOTES

1   This interview took place at Zentropa, in Copenhagen, on 11 August 2009.

2   The clear privileging of female characters is even more evident in *Melancholia* (2011), in which the character played by Kirsten Dunst seems to embody the pessimistic and destructive side of the filmmaker, whereas Charlotte Gainsbourg plays Claire, the sympathetic, helpful sister of Justine (Dunst), and a wife confronting the rationalistic arrogance of her husband.